Teach Yourself
GUITAR

Teach Yourself
GUITAR

Nick Freeth

ABBEYDALE PRESS

© 2004 Bookmart Limited

Published by Abbeydale Press
An imprint of
Bookmart Limited
Registered Number 2372865
Trading as Bookmart Limited
Blaby Road
Wigston
Leicester
LE18 4SE

ISBN 1 86147 127 0

Printed in Dubai

Designed, packaged and produced for Bookmart
by Stonecastle Graphics Limited

Text by Nick Freeth
Photography by Roddy Paine
Designed by Paul Turner and Sue Pressley
Edited by Philip de Ste. Croix
Diagrams by Malcolm Porter
Illustrations of musicians by Steve Crisp

10 9 8 7 6 5 4 3 2 1

Acknowledgements:
The author and publisher would like to thank the following
manufacturers for their kind assistance in supplying pictures for
this book:

© Marshall Amplification plc: pages 19 *(bottom left)*, 139 *(top)*.
© Roland Corporation: pages 23 *(bottom right)*, 136-137.
© TASCAM: page 135.
© Kaman Corporation: pages 138 *(top)*, 139 *(bottom)*.
© Laney Amplification: page 138 *(bottom)*.

Thanks also to Dave Cook of Abbey Music, Tunbridge Wells, Kent for
kindly supplying guitars and equipment for photography.

Contents

Introduction

Teach **Yourself Guitar** offers a beginners' guide to the techniques of guitar playing, and also explains a little about the workings of music itself. It will show you how to form chords and scales, pick and strum solo lines and rhythmic patterns – and help you to understand how these elements can be combined into songs and instrumentals, and written down as notation and tablature. No prior musical or theoretical knowledge is assumed, and as the book rarely refers to specific styles, it will be useful to you whatever genre you're interested in, and whether you want to play steel-strung acoustic or electric guitar.

Most of us read books and magazines at a steady, unchanging speed, and can therefore be fairly sure how long it'll take us to reach the end of a novel or an article. Your progress through *Teach Yourself Guitar* won't be quite so evenly paced; after swiftly absorbing its opening pages, which contain advice on choosing and buying an instrument, you may find the next few chapters slower going, as your hands struggle to accustom themselves to their unfamiliar fingering and strumming tasks.

Later on in the book, having developed some speed and co-ordination in picking and chording, you'll face the further challenge of relating what you play to dots and symbols on the page – a process demanding the seemingly impossible feat of concentrating on the neck, the plectrum and the notation at the same time! The only way to surmount such problems is through constant practice, which may involve spending weeks on certain sections of the book until its instructions and exercises become second nature. Though ultimately rewarding, this won't be especially quick or effortless...and any guitar tutor claiming to make it so is being less than honest with you.

Below: With the help of this book, you'll soon be strumming chords...

By the time you reach the final pages of *Teach Yourself Guitar*, however, you'll have surmounted these earlier difficulties, and will be ready to apply your playing skills to real music, instead of just scale passages and chord diagrams. Mastering this book's contents is, of course, only 'the end of the beginning' of truly learning the instrument. Think of it as the equivalent of a pilot's 'wings': a basic qualification, providing you with a solid foundation for your subsequent musical adventures. Where, and how far these take you depends on your talent, energy, and desire to expand your abilities. Good luck, and have fun!

Above: Learning to play the guitar is much easier with an instrument that feels comfortable as well as looking and sounding good.

Left: ...though it may take a little longer before you're ready for a jam session like this!

Chapter 1

Choosing a Guitar and Amp

Guitars, like motorbikes and other objects of desire, can cast a powerfully seductive spell over even the most level-headed and experienced of prospective buyers. As a beginner, with no practical knowledge of the models you see in the showroom, you're in danger of being swept off your feet – and into a disastrous purchase – by a gleaming, enticing instrument that may turn out to be quite unsuitable for you. The advice in this chapter should prevent you from making an expensive mistake when choosing your first 'axe': supplement it by taking a look though a few guitar magazines before you go to the music store, and – if possible – by bringing along a friend who already plays, and can provide some additional advice during the selection process. Don't allow yourself to be rushed or railroaded while making your choice; and avoid visiting guitar shops on a Saturday, when they tend to be at their busiest and noisiest.

The Acoustic Guitar

Acoustic and electric guitars are played in similar ways, and usually tuned identically. But while electrics generate sound with the help of built-in magnetic pickups, and must be connected to an amplifier to be heard properly, acoustics can boost and project the vibrations from their strings without any electronic assistance. There are several different kinds of acoustic guitar, including classical and flamenco instruments, 'archtops' with violin-like bodies, and models containing metal resonators. However, the most popular – and the one we'll be focusing on in this book – is the 'flat-top', favoured by a wide range of pop, rock, folk and blues musicians, and illustrated here.

Right: The author's 'parlour-style' Larrivée flat-top acoustic.

Flat-tops evolved from gut-strung classical guitars (see panel), but are much more strongly built than their Spanish-style cousins – largely because they have to withstand the tension of the steel strings that give them their bright, ringing tone. These are fastened to the instrument's **headstock** via a set of geared tuning pegs called **machine heads**. They then pass over a grooved block known as the **nut**, down the **neck** (faced with a **fingerboard** and metal **frets**), and across the guitar's **top** and **soundhole** to the **bridge**. This component transfers energy from the plucked strings to the top, and also anchors the string ends, which are pushed into holes behind its **saddle**, and held in place by wooden pins.

Flat-top types

The flat-top in our photograph is a small-size model, whose neck joins its body at the 12th fret, restricting access to some higher notes – a slight disadvantage outweighed, for many players, by the comfort, convenience and sweet sound offered by this style of instrument. Other guitarists prefer the warmer, more powerful timbre of bigger flat-tops (the largest are known as 'jumbos' or 'dreadnoughts'); these generally have 14 frets 'to the body'.

THE GUITAR'S EARLY HISTORY

The guitar first emerged in Spain during the 16th century, and soon spread throughout Europe. Originally a small-bodied instrument fitted with four or five 'courses' (pairs) of gut strings, its shape and configuration changed considerably over the next two hundred years. The most important single figure in its development was probably Antonio de Torres (1817-1892), the Spaniard who created the modern 'classical' guitar, and influenced many other craftsmen on both sides of the Atlantic. However, it was American-based companies – several of them, like Martin and Epiphone, founded by émigrés from Europe – who pioneered the concept of steel-strung guitars. These were loathed by purists (and are still shunned by today's classical and flamenco players), but were enthusiastically adopted by popular performers from the late 19th century onwards.

Left: The Larrivée's ebony bridge, with its cream-coloured saddle and dotted pins, is glued to the guitar's sitka spruce top.

Above: The instrument's headstock, machine heads and nut.

11

The Electric Guitar

The introduction of the electromagnetic pickup in the early 1930s enabled the quiet-voiced guitar to compete on equal terms with drums, saxophones, trumpets and other noisy musical rivals. It consisted of a magnet and a wire coil, both mounted close to the guitar's steel strings. When the strings were struck, their movement disturbed the field created by the magnet, and produced small electrical currents in the coil; these signals (which corresponded to the notes or chords being played) were then sent through a cable to an amplifier and loudspeaker. Today's pickups, though more compact and efficient than their bulky predecessors, work in a very similar way.

Right: A mid-price, Mexican-made Fender Telecaster.

Some players wanting to amplify their instruments simply add pickups to their existing acoustics, but better results are usually achieved by buying a 'real' electric guitar. These fall into four main categories: deep-bodied 'semi-acoustics' giving a mellow, jazzy sound; 'thinline' and 'semi-solid' designs with reduced internal cavities, offering some of the tonal warmth of a semi-acoustic in a slimmer, more manageable form; and 'solids' that completely dispense with the traditional hollow guitar body, replacing it with a wooden slab to which the instrument's neck, pickups and bridge are attached.

The 'Tele'

Our main photos show a classic solid model, the Fender Telecaster – a best seller that has been in continuous production for over 50 years. It has two pickups: one in the 'front' (neck) position, providing a soft timbre ideal for chord and rhythm playing; and a more powerful 'back' (bridge) pickup, often used for soloing. Either or both can be selected by the switch to the right of the bridge assembly; beneath it are volume and tone controls. The string ends pass through the bridge-plate and the body, and are anchored inside holes visible at the back of the instrument. The socket for the amplifier lead is set into the guitar's side.

12

Left: A close up showing the Telecaster's pickups, bridge and controls. Its lower ('back') pickup is angled to boost the treble response.

Left: This ingeniously designed socket helps to keep the instrument's connecting cable out of the player's way.

Above: An inexpensive three-pickup 'axe' that would be an ideal guitar for a beginner.

Choosing an Acoustic

Selecting your first acoustic is far from easy, and you will need guidance from a reputable guitar dealer to help you make the right choice. Find a friendly, well-stocked store, and ask to look at some steel-strung, flat-top acoustics suitable for beginners – preferably in a range of sizes and types. The cheapest will have laminated tops and bodies; these are made from thin layers of higher quality wood, bonded to strips of inferior timber. At the next level are models with solid tops, but laminated backs and sides: a top carved from solid spruce or cedar will always sound better than its plywood rivals, though this improvement comes at a price. The finest acoustic guitars have all-solid tops, backs and sides, and their superior tone can be expected to mellow further with age.

Above: The distance between strings and fingerboard on this acoustic will suit most players; electrics may have their action set a little lower.

Which should you choose? The answer depends on your preferences and your budget. Ask the salesperson, or a guitar-playing friend, to demonstrate the instruments – and while you're listening and comparing, examine each model and work through the checklist on the panel opposite.

Trying out your guitar

Your responses to this, and your reaction to the sound of the instruments, should narrow your selection down to a 'shortlist' of two or three. Take a seat, place each of the 'finalists' on your right thigh, and position your hands on the guitar as shown in the photograph. (See the panel a little further on if you're left-handed.) Press one or two of the strings down onto the fingerboard with your left-hand index finger – first near the nut, then further up the neck. If they seem a long way above the fingerboard (see detail photograph), and it's an effort to hold them down, try a model with lower **action** – ask the assistant about this. Also, recheck each guitar's size and weight: which feels the most comfortable, and balances best?

Right: An attractive, laminated-wood flat-top guitar, made in the Far East, and ideal for learrners on a tight budget.

14

ACOUSTIC GUITAR CHECKLIST

Is the guitar well finished?

Check for:

• Cracks

• Superficial damage to the varnish or wood

• Chisel-marks on the neck and body

• Rough-edged frets (run your hand gently along the sides of the fingerboard to spot these)

• Dried glue around the nut

• Dried glue inside the body (use a small torch to see inside the soundhole)

• Loose or crooked machine heads and bridge pins

Is its neck straight?

A guitar with a warped or twisted neck is hard to play, and will have bad intonation. Check by looking along the neck – if you're at all uncertain about it, ask the assistant, or choose another instrument

Does it rattle or buzz while it's being played?

If so, ask the assistant to find out what may be causing these noises

Do you like its shape and colour?

You'll be spending a lot of time with the instrument you buy, so, as well as sounding good, its contours and finish need to please you visually

Pick the guitar up and hold it against your body.

Does it feel well balanced and comfortable, or is it too large and heavy for you?

The acoustic that scores highest in these tests, and has the most pleasing tone, is the one for you – if you can afford it! While you're in the shop, consider buying a spare set of strings, some picks in various shapes and sizes, and a case for your instrument, if it doesn't already have one.

Left: Hold the guitar like this to find out how it feels in your hands.

Above: For some players, the position seen here – with the instrument resting on the left thigh – gives the best balance and comfort.

Choosing an Electric

Most of the points mentioned on the previous pages also apply to buying an electric guitar – though there are several additional factors to consider when choosing one. If you're tempted by classic American designs like Gibson's Les Paul, or Fender's Telecaster and Stratocaster, it's worth knowing that these and other famous Gibson and Fender 'axes' are available at several different quality and price levels. Gibson sells top-grade, US-built Les Pauls under its own name, and budget versions branded as Epiphones; while Fender makes inexpensive 'Squier' Teles and Strats, plus Fender-badged models originating (in ascending order of cost) from Mexico, Japan and California. There are few visual differences between the 'economy' and 'premium' versions, though better materials, components and workmanship are found on the costlier instruments.

However, don't restrict your shortlist to American-designed guitars. There are a growing number of fine European electrics on the market, while Asian manufacturers are also known for their superb, value-for-money instruments, which include some strikingly original models. A few of these have unusual body shapes, and extras like elaborate tremolo systems (see photo right); make sure such features don't affect the guitar's balance, or make it uncomfortable to hold when sitting down.

Trying out your axe

Obviously, you must audition the models you're considering through an amplifier. When the music store assistant demonstrates them, check that the amp is set at medium volume, with no treble or bass boost from its tone controls, and no electronic effects (such as 'reverb' or chorusing) selected. Ask to hear the output from the individual pickups on each instrument (units mounted nearer the fingerboard will have a bassier, less

Left: The contoured body
on this solid electric makes
it especially comfortable
to hold and play.

cutting sound than those closer to the bridge), and when assessing their tone, also listen out for excessive hum, noise, electrical interference, or 'breakthough' from radio signals.

As well as spare strings, picks, pitch pipes and a case, you need two other items: an amplifier (see following pages); and a connecting lead – this should be at least 10 feet (3m) long, with robust screening, and well-made jack-plugs.

Left: Many electrics – even cheaper models like this one – have 'whammy bars' that allow you to bend the pitch of their strings.

LEFT-HANDERS AND THE GUITAR

Most left-handed players prefer to use their right hands to fret the guitar's strings, and will need to buy restrung instruments with modified bodies, bridges and nuts, altered internal bracing (on acoustics) and changes to the pickup configuration (on electrics). Some manufacturers produce these at no extra cost, but others charge as much as 10 per cent extra for them.

When forming chords and scales, left-handers' finger positions on the neck are 'mirror images' of those used by right-handed players – though the actual fingers assigned to each string (1st, 2nd etc.) are unchanged.

Right: Unlike most left-handers, Jimi Hendrix usually played right-handed guitars, turning over their bodies and 'reverse-stringing' them – a method that places body cutaways and pickup controls the 'wrong' way up!

The Amplifier

Amplifiers and loudspeakers are an integral part of any electric guitarist's set-up, not only boosting, but shaping and modifying the output from the instrument's pickups. Unlike hi-fi and studio equipment, which boasts an even ('flat') frequency response and minimal levels of distortion and coloration, guitar amps are specifically designed to emphasize areas of the audio spectrum that enhance the guitar's sound, and – when required – to generate overloads and other 'impurities' for musical effect. They must also be robust enough to withstand a degree of rough handling, as well as long periods of operation at high volume.

Most guitarists prefer valve-driven amplifiers, whose warm, creamy tone can easily be nudged into singing sustain and rich, throaty distortion. However, valve amps are often bulky and expensive (the Kustom 12A shown here is a rare exception), and cheaper, transistorized models, which can sound almost as good as their 'tube'-powered counterparts, may be more convenient and practical for some players – especially beginners. Nearly all solid-state amps are supplied as 'combos', incorporating one or two built-in loudspeakers; valve amps are also available in combo form, or as separate units which are paired with speaker cabinets to create 'stacks'.

Amp power and speaker size

When buying an amp, always check its rated power output in **watts RMS** (root mean square); other forms of measurement sometimes used by manufacturers and dealers are misleading, and should be ignored. Remember that a more powerful amp is likely to perform better – even at quiet volumes – than a lower-rated one, and that transistorized units delivering less than 30 watts RMS may struggle to handle anything much more demanding than

practice sessions. (Modestly specified valve amps tend to provide rather higher outputs – models of as little as 10 watts can pack a considerable punch.) Also ensure that the loudspeaker fitted to your combo is at least 8in (20.3cm) in diameter – anything smaller won't do justice to your guitar's lower notes.

Above: A lightweight, compact, solid-state guitar combo.

Below: The Kustom Tube 12A is probably the smallest, cheapest valve amp currently available.

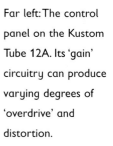

Far left: The control panel on the Kustom Tube 12A. Its 'gain' circuitry can produce varying degrees of 'overdrive' and distortion.

Left: Your amp plays a key role in determining your overall sound – make sure you choose one that brings out the best in your axe.

Left: A classic 'stack' from Marshall, the British company that first created the concept in the 1960s. It comprises a 100-watt JCM800 valve amp, and two 'cabs', each containing four 12in (30.5cm) speakers.

19

Chapter 2
Basic Playing Skills

Your decision to become a guitarist was almost certainly fuelled by fantasies of being able to produce breathtaking solos from your axe with a minimum of study and practice – and now, as you gaze at your new instrument, you probably wish you knew some instant magic formula that would allow you to play it with the effortless virtuosity you already achieve in your dreams.

In reality, of course, learning the guitar isn't so swift and straightforward, as you'll discover on the next few pages, which outline a range of basic technical skills that need to be absorbed so thoroughly that they become second nature to you. This process takes time and patience; but as you coax your hands into unfamiliar new positions, and suffer the discomfort of sore fingertips and aching muscles, you can be confident that your hard work is taking you, slowly but surely, towards your ultimate goal of guitar mastery.

Tuning Up

Having got your guitar back home and unpacked it, you're probably impatient to start playing; but there's a preliminary task to master first – getting the instrument 'in tune'. This involves verifying the pitch of its strings against a reliable external source, such as a **piano** or **synthesizer keyboard**, **pitch pipes**, or a dedicated **electronic tuner**.

Whichever one you choose, have it within easy reach when you sit down to tune up. (We'll give more detailed consideration to your posture on the next two pages.) If you've got an electric guitar, plug its lead into your amp *before* switching the power on; this avoids generating electronic thumps that can damage your loudspeaker cone. Set the amp's overall volume to a low-to-medium level, turn up the volume on your guitar to about 75 per cent, and select the bridge (back) pickup – its brighter tone will make tuning easier.

Your guitar has six strings; the thinnest, highest-pitched of them is named the *first* or numbered *1*, the next one down is the *second*, and so on. Each is **tuned** to a specific **note** often referred to by a letter of the alphabet. (Don't be intimidated by the initially mysterious terms used for notes and other musical technicalities – this book will guide you through them.) Here's a list of the guitar's standard string pitches, and a diagram showing where they can be found on the keyboard.

• The 1st string is tuned to the E two 'white notes' above **middle C** on the keyboard
• The 2nd string is tuned to the B three 'white notes' below this E on the keyboard (one white note below middle C)
• The 3rd string is tuned to the G two 'white notes' below the B
• The 4th string is tuned to the D three 'white notes' below the G
• The 5th string is tuned to the A three 'white notes' below the D
• The 6th string is tuned to the E three 'white notes' below the A

Tuning to a keyboard

When tuning your guitar to a piano, first check that it's at **concert pitch** (see glossary), or, better still, use a digital keyboard; these never drift out of tune.

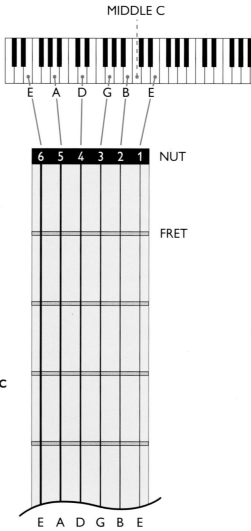

Find the E key corresponding to the guitar's 1st string: strike it, then immediately pluck the top E string with a right-hand finger or a pick (see picture right).

If the two pitches are identical, the string is in tune. If the string's note is *lower* than the piano's (the musical term for this is **flat**), keep comparing them, while slowly tightening the string by turning its machine head with your left hand (see picture below).

As the two pitches converge, you may notice a 'beating' effect that will disappear once they match exactly. If the string is **sharp**

(too high in pitch) relative to the keyboard, slacken it instead of tightening it; once it's set correctly, tune the other five strings in the same way.

Tuning to pitch pipes

If you're using pitch pipes, hold them in your left hand or your mouth, and blow each reed while picking and adjusting the strings as explained above (see picture below left).

Using an electronic tuner

Electronic tuners give you a highly accurate visual indication (via a built-in meter or digital display) of the pitch of your guitar strings, so you don't need to rely on your 'ear' when tuning with them. They have built-in microphones, as well as input sockets for electric instruments, and can often be permanently connected between guitar and amp to provide tuning checks whenever they're required.

Below: A reliable, battery-operated electronic tuner suitable for both acoustic and electric instruments.

23

Preparing to Play

Now you're in tune, take a moment to get comfortable and organized before you start playing in earnest. If you've been sitting near a piano or synth keyboard, consider moving away from it to give yourself more space, and check your surroundings for other potential obstacles – especially sharp-edged furniture that could damage the finish of your guitar in an accidental collision! Ideally, the area where you practise should contain nothing much more than an upright chair with good back support and no arms, and a music stand or similar rest for this book.

Right: The 'classical' way of holding a guitar: poised, comfortable – but not very 'rock and roll'!

When you sit down to play, your guitar should be balanced securely on one of your thighs, with its neck pointing slightly upwards. Your left hand must be able to move up and down the fingerboard without strain or discomfort, and ought not to have to 'hold on' to keep the instrument in place. Your right hand fingers should be roughly parallel to the strings: try not to rest your right wrist on the bridge, as this can deaden the sound, and affect the striking angle of your pick or fingers, spoiling your tone. Resist the temptation to practise standing up – at least for now: it may look good, but it causes additional complications that will impede your progress.

The photographs show four basic postures commonly used by seated guitarists. The 'classical' method (top right), with a footstool often raising the leg that supports the instrument, ensures optimum freedom of movement for both hands – but most non-classical players prefer the more relaxed postures seen in the other photos, in which the guitar is held either on the right thigh, or on the left thigh crossed over the right.

Right: This cross-legged posture raises the left thigh, giving good balance and support.

24

Nails and fingertips

Finally, examine the state of your left-hand fingernails. These must be kept as short as possible; long nails will prevent you from holding down notes and chords properly, and may leave scratches on the surface of your fingerboard. Even such elegantly taloned performers as Dolly Parton trim their nails before doing any serious playing; it's a regrettable, but essential, sacrifice that all guitarists have to make. It's also only fair to give you advance warning of the soreness and inflammation your left-hand fingertips will suffer once they're exposed to the pressures of fretting – although, thanks to modern guitars' lower action and lighter string gauges, this problem is not as severe as it once was. Fortunately, after a few weeks, you'll develop thick calluses on the parts of your fingers that make contact with the strings, and will be able to reach for the most demanding chords without so much as a twinge of pain!

Above: Guitarists' left-hand nails should be short, and free from splits and jagged edges.

Left: This easy, informal playing position is widely used by non-classical guitarists.

Above: Another comfortable, well-balanced way of holding your guitar.

Basic Picking

While tuning up, we didn't pay much attention to the correct way in which to strike the strings, but now we're about to do something more musical on the guitar, it's important to learn a few simple right-hand techniques that will help you produce as clean and rich a tone as possible.

Initially, we're going to focus on playing with a **pick** (also known as a **flat-pick** or a **plectrum**) rather than separate right-hand fingers. Picks are preferred by most guitarists for their precision, and the crisp, percussive sound they create; they're made in various shapes and thicknesses, but all have a slightly pointed end that's used to make contact with the strings. Hold your pick between the thumb and index finger of your right hand; the pick should be kept straight, with about a centimetre between your grip and its tip. Now position your right wrist and

hand over the guitar's strings as shown in the first photograph, and place the pick just above and behind the 4th (D) string. Move your hand downwards from your wrist (try to keep your forearm fairly still and relaxed), strike the open (unfretted) 4th string with the tip of the pick, and stop before it reaches the 3rd (G) string (see pictures and diagram).

Practise **downstrokes** (the technical term for what we've just done) on this single string until you can sound it without catching the pick on it, or accidentally

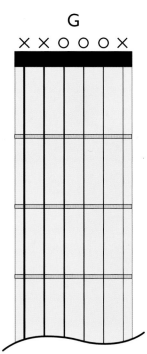

G

X X O O O X

Above: We'll be featuring guitar neck diagrams like this throughout the book to show you which strings (and, later, fingerings) to use for chords. An 'x' above a string means that you shouldn't strike it; an 'o' indicates that it should be played open (unfretted). The chord's name (G) is printed at the top of the diagram.

Left: Preparing to play a note – the pick moves down towards the open D (4th) string…

striking adjacent strings. Try picking more and less vigorously, and listen to the resultant changes in the volume and tone, but avoid using excessive force, which can cause buzzes, thumps and other unmusical noises if the string collides with the frets. As you play, you'll probably find yourself instinctively holding onto the instrument's neck with your left hand. Avoid doing this; instead, let your left arm fall to your side, allowing your right forearm and thigh to keep the guitar in position.

Once you're happy with the sound you're producing, have a go at your first chord (a basic version of G major – we'll be looking at how chords are named on the next few pages) by striking the open 4th (D), 3rd (G), and 2nd (B) strings in succession, using a single downstroke, and leaving all three notes to resonate once you've picked them. (It's all too easy to deaden their vibrations with your right hand – make sure this is kept well clear of the strings). Start by striking slowly, and then increase the speed of your downstrokes until the three notes are being sounded almost simultaneously. This faster playing of adjacent strings is called **strumming**; it's one of the most important of all guitar techniques, and we'll soon be exploring it in more detail.

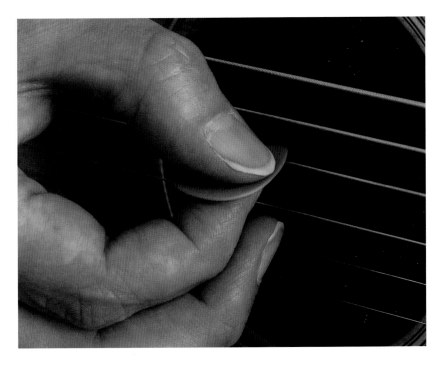

Left: …and strikes it.

Below: The pick comes to rest after sounding the last note (B) of the three-string G chord.

Open Strings and Fretted Notes

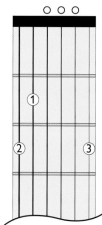

G

A s you've just discovered, strumming involves using one sweep of the pick to play strings that lie next to each other. The more notes you can strike at once, the richer your chords will sound – and it's easy to build up four-, five- and six-note harmonies on the guitar by using combinations of open and fretted strings.

Left: The chord of G in diagram form. Only the first three fret positions are illustrated; circled numbers on the 'string' lines show which fingers to use for each note.

Let's start by giving an extra top note to the open D (4th), G (3rd) and B (2nd) chord that you've already learned. This will come from the 1st string, which is tuned to E, but can provide us with a G if it's pressed down behind the 3rd fret on the neck (see photo). Try doing this with the third finger on your left hand; it may not seem the most convenient digit to use, but you'll soon understand why we've chosen it. Place its tip on the 1st string, in the middle of the space between the 2nd and 3rd frets, and rest the base of your thumb on the back of the neck – or at its side, as shown in the photo opposite – to provide support. Avoid tensing up, or grasping the neck too tightly. Press your fingertip down onto the string, holding it against the wood of the fingerboard; keep the top part of your finger at a right angle to the neck, and don't allow it to touch the adjacent B (2nd) string. Now take the pick in your right hand, and strike the fretted G. Does the note it produces sound clean, or is it buzzing and choking as you struggle to hold the string down? If you're having trouble, make sure the nail on your left-hand finger isn't getting in the way (see previous comments). You may also find that pressure on the string makes your fingertip sore; if this happens, take a brief rest before trying the note again.

Above: Holding down the 1st string at the 3rd fret to produce a G. The placing of the other fingers isn't critical at this stage – so long as they don't get in the way of the remaining strings!

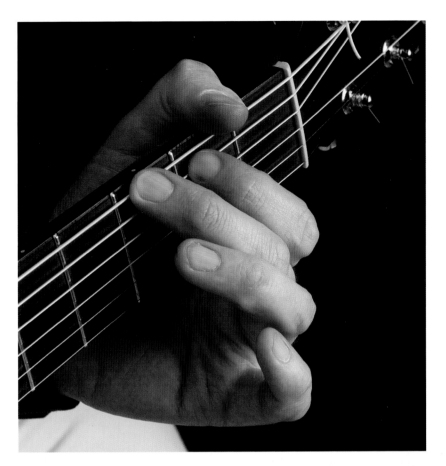

Once you've mastered the fretting process, strum the guitar's top four strings with the pick. The results are resonant and pleasing, but the lowest note, the open D on the 4th string, leaves the chord sounding unsatisfying and incomplete. We can remedy this by adding a new bottom note – a bass G from the 6th string, fretted at the 3rd fret – while enhancing the texture even further with a B from the 2nd fret of the 5th string. Use your second finger on the 6th, and your index finger for the 5th; keep them upright so they don't touch any neighbouring strings. You may find the full six-string chord shape rather a stretch at first; if so, leave out the 1st string G until you've sorted out any other buzzes or partially sounding notes.

Left: Two new notes for our G chord: G and B. These are fretted by the second and first fingers on the 6th and 5th strings, while the third finger moves towards the 'top' G on the 1st string.

Above: Left-hand fingering for the complete, six-string G chord.

Right: Hold the fretted notes down firmly, but make sure your second and first fingers don't accidentally touch the strings to their right.

Major and Minor Chords

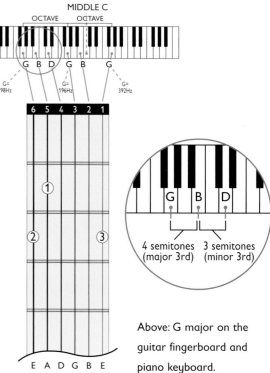

After strumming your chord, try sounding its six individual notes more slowly, starting with the lowest (6th) string and ending with the 1st. Then, using separate downstrokes, play the 6th, followed by the open 3rd, and the 1st. The three notes, which share the same name, G, closely resemble each other, and there's a simple scientific explanation for their similarity: each vibrates at a **frequency** (measured in **cycles per second** or **Hertz**) exactly twice the pitch of its predecessor. The low G on the fretted 6th string is measured at 98Hz, while the 3rd string G vibrates at 196Hz, and the 1st string G at 392Hz; you may be able to check these figures on an electronic guitar tuner, if you have one.

Above: G major on the guitar fingerboard and piano keyboard.

Musicians describe notes related in this way as being in **octaves**; the term comes from the Latin word for 'eight', and the three Gs in your chord each lie eight white notes apart (counting inclusively from G to G) on the piano keyboard, as shown on the diagram opposite. To locate another octave **interval** in the chord, pick the 5th and 2nd strings, which are both Bs; the remaining note (the open D on the 4th string) has no octave 'double'.

As we've demonstrated, adding the two additional Gs and the 5th string B makes our chord sound fuller and thicker. But such duplications don't alter its basic ingredients, which are simply G, B and D. From the inset diagram, you can see that there are four black and white piano key 'steps' between G (the 'root' or 'home' note of the chord) and B, and three separating B and D. Musicians call these steps **semitones** (see panel), and describe a four-semitone gap as a **major third**. The presence of this interval between

the root G and B defines our chord as **major**, and because chords are usually named after their root notes, this one is known as **G major** (or simply **G**).

By contrast, **minor** chords have only *three* semitones (a **minor third**) separating their first two notes – a smaller interval that creates a noticeably more melancholy mood. The easiest of all minors to play on the guitar is E minor, which uses even more open strings than the G chord you've already mastered. Its bass or root (E) is provided by the open 6th string, and its top three notes (G, B, and E) come from the unfretted 3rd, 2nd and 1st. We'll fill it out with a B from the 5th string, and an E from the adjacent 4th string; these are held down at the second fret by (respectively) your second and third fingers. Remember to keep them at 90° to the neck, and don't allow them to touch the open 6th or 3rd strings. Once you've positioned your left hand correctly, strum all the strings, and relish the result!

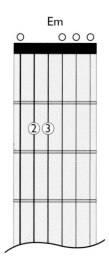

Above: The E minor chord's four open strings give it an especially rich, ringing tone.

Fingering and picking the chord of E minor.

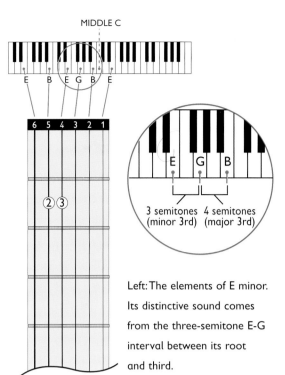

MIDDLE C

E   B   E   G   B   E

6 5 4 3 2 1

② ③

E   G   B

3 semitones   4 semitones
(minor 3rd)   (major 3rd)

Left: The elements of E minor. Its distinctive sound comes from the three-semitone E-G interval between its root and third.

SEMITONES AND NOTE NAMES

The semitone is the smallest 'officially' recognized interval in standard Western music. Adjacent piano keys produce notes a semitone apart; while on the guitar, each fret corresponds to a semitone, and the pitch from its strings rises by semitone steps as the player's left hand moves up the fingerboard, stopping them at successively higher positions.

An octave consists of 12 semitones, which are identified using a recurring cycle of note names taken from the first seven letters of the alphabet, augmented by the terms **sharp** (#) and **flat** (♭). A sharpened note is *raised* by a semitone, and a flattened one is *lowered* by the same amount. (For reasons explained later, sharp and flat notes are sometimes given alternative names – B♭ can be called A#, C# can be D♭, etc.) The diagram on the right shows the position of these semitone pitches on the piano keyboard, and at the first five frets of the guitar neck.

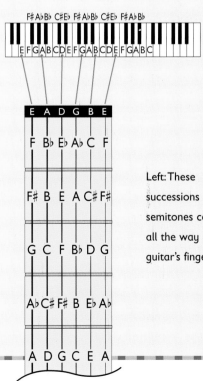

F# A♭ B♭ C# E♭ F# A♭ B♭ C# E♭ F# A♭ B♭

E F G A B C D E F G A B C D E F G A B C

E A D G B E

F   B♭   E♭   A♭   C   F

F#   B   E   A   C#   F#

G   C   F   B♭   D   G

A♭ C# F# B E♭ A♭

A   D   G   C   E   A

Left: These successions of semitones continue all the way up the guitar's fingerboard.

Basic Harmonies for G Major and C Major

The six-string versions of G major and E minor you've just learned are two of the most widely encountered chords in guitar music, where they're often combined with a pair of other 'favourites', C major and D major. The finger positions for the new shapes are illustrated in the photograph and on the diagram opposite. Note the Xs shown above the 6th string on the C shape, and above the 6th and 5th on the D. They tell you that the marked strings shouldn't be sounded; when playing the C chord, you should start your pick stroke from the fretted C on the 5th string, and begin the D chord with the open 4th (D) string.

At first, getting your left-hand fingers to fret these chords will be a slow, painful process, and you'll find that it takes even longer to shift from shape to shape. The only way to overcome discomfort and build up fluency is by constant practice, which will eventually make switching between chords second nature. However, you can speed up the assimilation process by 'visualizing' your finger movements when you're away from the instrument, and even miming them, 'air-guitar' style – though you'll probably want to do this when no one else is watching!

As you strum G, E minor, C and D in succession, you'll find that the sequence of harmonies carries echoes and hints of countless pop songs. Try them in a different order (say, G, D, E minor, C, then back to G), and they'll remind you of other familiar numbers. You'll also begin to notice how the chords relate to one another. Going from G to D is a little like starting a sentence and leaving it hanging in mid-air; and passing through C and E minor only intensifies the

musical 'longing' to return to G, which seems to be the 'home' chord of the four. We'll study the technicalities behind these subjective effects in more detail later; for now, all you need to know is that the chords you've been playing are the basic harmonies for the **key** of G major; and that other keys use their own chords in exactly the same way to create the sensations of musical tension and release you've been experiencing.

Above: C major: a relatively easy chord, as the third, second and first fingers fall naturally into its shape.

Chords for G major

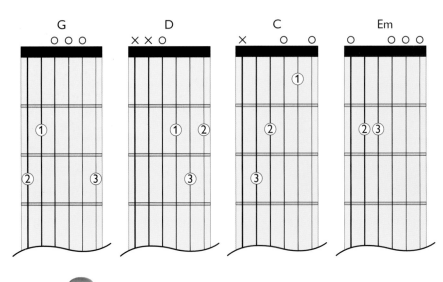

To demonstrate this, let's explore the four basic chords for C major. You already know two of them: C (the 'home' chord in the new key) and G; they're combined with A minor and F – a shape that poses a particular challenge, as it requires you to fret two notes (the F at the 1st fret/1st string, and the C on the 1st fret/2nd string) simultaneously with your left-hand index finger. Flatten it across the two strings (see photo below right), and then press it down, while keeping your second and third fingers in their usual, right-angled position relative to the neck. Once you can play these four chords cleanly, strum them in different combinations (as you did with the G major chords) and listen to the way they work together.

Chords for C major

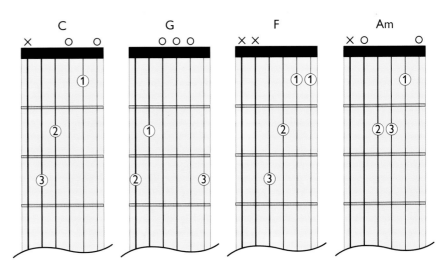

Above: The placing of the third finger on the 3rd fret/2nd string for the D chord takes a little getting used to.

Above right: A minor. Note that the little finger, though close to the 1st string, is not actually touching it.

Right: F major, with the index finger holding down both the 1st and 2nd strings at the 1st fret.

33

Upstrokes and Downstrokes

Right: The 'Westminster Chimes' exercise begins with a downstroke on the open G string.

Centre: Having just played the second note in the first group of 'chimes' (open B), the pick is now travelling upwards towards the 3rd string to strike the A.

The last few pages have concentrated on chords, and the development of basic left-hand techniques; we've focused rather less on your right hand, and it's now time to remedy this.

So far, you've been using only downstrokes while strumming and picking, but in order to play more easily and rapidly, you need to learn how to strike the strings in the opposite direction with **upstrokes**. To see how valuable these can be, we'll try a very simple, single-string exercise, based on the 'Westminster Chimes' sounded from the clock tower above London's Houses of Parliament. The piece uses only three strings (the 4th, 3rd and 2nd): let's start by playing it solely with downstrokes. This diagram shows you where to find the four notes for the exercise, and the list below it gives the order in which they should be struck.

These four pitches comprise the 'Westminster Chimes'. Three of them (D, G and B) come from open strings (indicated by circles over the 'nut' on the diagram); the other, A, should be held down by your second finger on the 2nd fret/3rd string.

Play the notes in this order, with short gaps between each set of four.

G	B	A	D
G	A	B	G
B	G	A	D
D	A	B	G

By now, you should be having little difficulty in picking the strings cleanly, but you're probably finding that moving the plectrum back up to its 'pre-strike' position between each note feels rather awkward. Play the exercise again, using both down- and upstrokes, as indicated on the second 'grid' of note letters below.

The lower-case 'd' or 'u' above each note indicates a down- or upstroke.

d	u	u	u
G	B	A	D

u	d	u	u
G	A	B	G

u	d	u	d
B	G	A	D

d	d	d	u
D	A	B	G

The strokes shown here will reduce the movement of your pick and right hand to a minimum. 'For example: it makes sense to play the first 'chime' in the initial group of notes with a downstroke, but then use upstrokes for the next three notes, as the strings required for these are adjacent, and your pick can strike them, one after the other, on a single upward arc. When sounding the open B, simply reverse the direction of your pick, and the A and D (2nd

Above: Preparing for an open B downstroke for the penultimate note of the final group of 'chimes'.

fret/3rd string and open 4th string) will fall naturally beneath it as your hand moves away from the floor (see photos). At first, you may find upstrokes hard to control; practise getting them to match the attack and volume generated by your downstrokes.

Upstrokes are also very useful in when playing chords, allowing you to replace simple downstroke strumming with more interesting effects. Here's a short G major chord sequence, in which each new chord is sounded three times: first with a downstroke, then with an upstroke, and finally with a second downstroke. On the downstrokes, strum the full chords – but on the upstrokes, strike just the top three strings, and allow the note(s) below them to continue ringing.

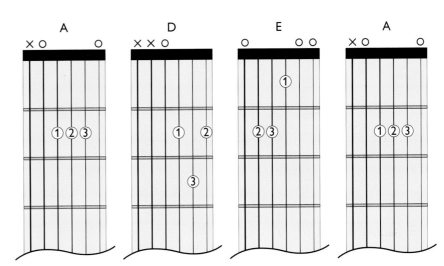

Below: Watch out for 'X'ed strings like those in the C and D chords here – remember not to strike these when you strum.

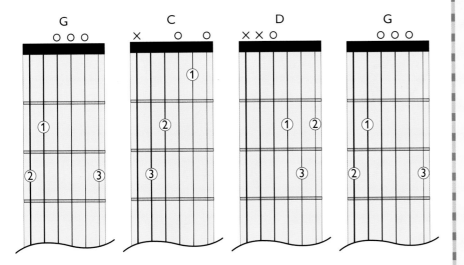

Try the same 'down-up-down' technique on these chords in D (below) and A major (top right), and also experiment with it when using other four-, five- and six-string shapes.

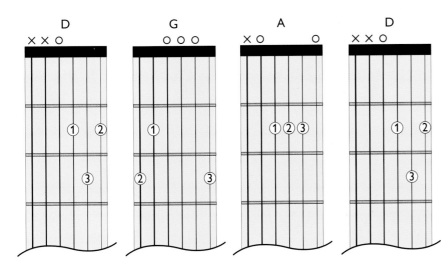

CHECKING YOUR TUNING

After a few hours of vigorous picking, you may find that the chords you play start to sound sour and jarring as your instrument slips out of tune. All six strings may have drifted out (usually flat) relative to the external source you originally tuned to (see earlier); or you may find that just a few of them need a little adjustment. If only small 'tweaks' seem to be required, try this simple method of comparing the pitches of neighbouring strings:

i) Ensure that the 1st (E) string is in tune using a pitch pipe, piano or tuner.
ii) Fret the 2nd (B) string at the 5th fret, pick it, and then strike the open 1st string. Their pitches should be exactly the same; if they aren't, adjust the 2nd to match the 1st.
iii) Compare the open 2nd and fretted 3rd string, remembering to fret the 3rd at the 4th fret to play a B. When retuning, always alter the lower of the two strings!
iv) Check the 3rd and 4th, 4th and 5th and 5th and 6th, fretting the lower string of each pair at the 5th fret.
v) Play a couple of chords: are they in tune? If not, try and work out which string(s) are sharp or flat; correct them, and then test again.

Shifted Shapes and the Capo

As you've probably noticed, most of the chords shown so far feature at least one of the guitar's open strings. Relying on these obviously restricts the range of harmonies at your disposal, ruling out any chord that doesn't include the notes E, A, D, G or B. However, once you 'escape' from the open strings, and start using just fretted notes for chords, many new possibilities are revealed.

Let's look a little more closely at the only non-open string shapes you know at present: F, B minor, and F sharp minor. All three can be slid up the fingerboard to create higher-pitched chords; each fret position corresponds to a semitone, so shifting the F shape up two frets (see photograph and diagram 1) produces a four-string chord of G; and raising it two more frets will transform it into an A.

Why would you want to do this? After all, you've already learned perfectly good versions of G and A! The answer lies in the contrasting sounds and alternative distribution of notes offered by the new chords. Our original, open-string A shape (see previous two pages) contained A, E, A, C# and E, while the four-string one gives us A, C#, E and a higher A: strum them one after the other and the difference will be clear. Now try moving the barréd F# minor shape three frets up the neck (see photo and diagram 2). In this position, it becomes A minor. Once again, compare it with the 'old' A minor shape a few pages earlier to appreciate the special qualities of each chord. For an even more striking demonstration of the same effect, play the shapes in diagram 3

and its associated photograph – a 'standard' six-string E minor, followed by the four-string version produced when you move the 'B minor' shape five frets up.

The capo – a flexible friend

Further on, we'll see how other chords can be similarly 'shifted', using more advanced left-hand fingering techniques. But if you're keen to explore the upper reaches of the neck with the shapes you're currently familiar with, try experimenting with a **capo** (see photograph opposite). This mechanical clamp (various types are available, usually costing no more than a few pounds) acts as a kind of surrogate nut, fretting all six strings at once, and making it easy to play in more remote keys and neck positions while still using simple fingerings. Attaching it at the first fret converts the open strings from E, A, D, G, B and E to F, B flat, E flat, A flat, C and F, and turns a standard C shape to C sharp, a D to E flat, and so on; each time you move the capo a fret further up, the string pitches (and your chords) are raised another semitone.

Above: The 'F' shape shifted up two frets to produce a chord of G.

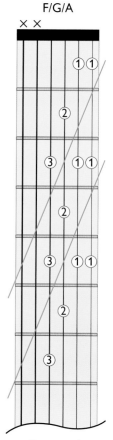

Diagram 1

Above: Our 'F# minor' fingering gives us an A minor chord when its barré is moved to the 5th fret position.

Rght: It's a long way up to this E minor chord, created by moving a 'B minor-type' shape to the 7th, 8th and 9th frets.

F#m/Am

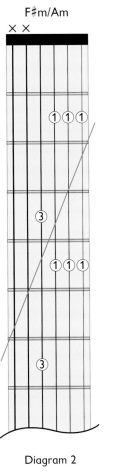

Diagram 2

Em/Em

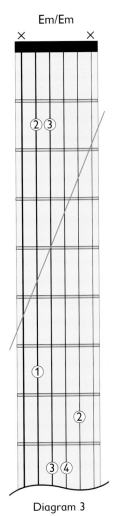

Diagram 3

Above: With the capo in place at the 1st fret, a standard 'E minor' chord becomes an F minor.

Minor Key Chords

You've now practised strumming and chord changing in the major keys of C, G, D and A, among whose basic harmonies are 'relative minor' chords: A minor for C, E minor for G, B minor for D, and F sharp minor for A. The root notes of these minors – A, E, B and F sharp – are the starting point for the **minor keys** and scales that bear their names; let's learn some more about the principal chords associated with each of them.

We'll begin with the 'three-chords plus one' for **A minor**. As well as A minor itself, which you're already familiar with, these include E major (it may seem surprising that minor keys use major chords so prominently; we'll be examining the reasons for this later) and D minor (see diagram) – a new shape, similar to the D major chord you've encountered previously, but with an F instead of an F sharp at the 1st string. The other main chord in the key is C major, A minor's **relative major** (see glossary).

The root chord of **E minor**, and its relative major, G, are old friends by now; the key also features A minor, as well as B major. The simplest way to play B is by modifying the fingerings we've formerly applied to A major. Start by placing your second, third and fourth fingers on (respectively) the 4th, 3rd and 2nd strings at the 2nd fret. Now slide all three fingers up to the 4th fret, before reaching 'behind' them with your index, which frets the root B on the 5th string/2nd fret (see photograph). Like the shapes we experimented with on the last two pages, this four-string chord (the 1st and 6th strings are not sounded) can be shifted around the neck to create other harmonies.

There is only one new chord (F sharp major – simply a four-string 'F major' fingering slid up a fret) needed for our next minor key, **B**

minor; and, as you'll observe from the diagrams below, the 'shiftable' A/B shape you've just learned is required again for C sharp major, one of the main chords in **F sharp minor**. Here, your index finger moves to the 4th fret on the 5th string, while the other three digits form a line, two frets higher, on the 4th, 3rd and 2nd strings.

Try strumming and changing between the chords in all these four keys. Like their major-key cousins, they'll soon start reminding you of well-known songs and tunes – and will make you keener than ever to apply your basic guitar-playing skills to some 'real' musical tasks. We'll start to do this in the next chapter; in the meantime, be patient – and keep practising!

Above: These pictures show a D major chord, and (below it) the altered fingering needed to change it to D minor.

Chords for A minor

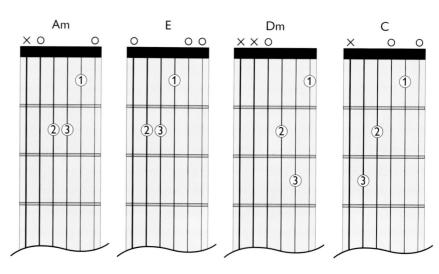

Chords for E minor

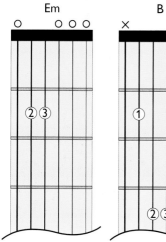
Em

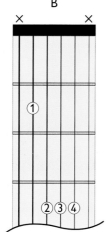
B

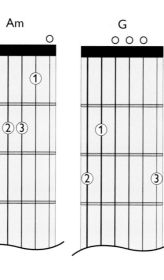
Am

G

Chords for B minor

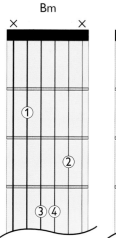
Bm

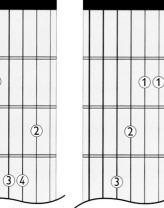
F#

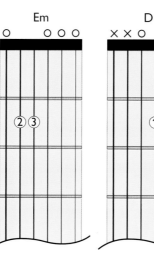
Em

D

Chords for F# minor

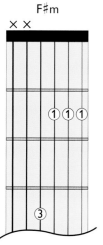
F#m

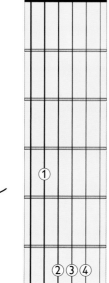
C#

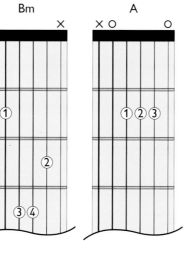
Bm

A

Above: This B major shape may be rather a stretch for players with smaller hands!

Right: Here, the 'B-type' shape seen in the previous photograph is moved up two frets to create a chord of C# major.

41

What You've Learned

* The highest of the guitar's six strings (the **1st**) is tuned to the E a **major 3rd** above 'middle C' on the piano; the other five, lower-pitched strings are tuned (in descending order) to B, G, D, A and E. The 6th string E lies two **octaves** below the E on the 1st string.

* Each of the guitar's frets corresponds to a **semitone** interval, which is also the difference in pitch between two adjacent piano keys. A note from an unfretted or 'open' string is raised by a semitone if the string is pressed onto the fingerboard behind the 1st fret; holding it down behind the 2nd fret increases its pitch by a further semitone, and so on.

* Notes created by groups of unfretted and/or fretted strings form **chords**; when the strings producing them are next to each other, they can be **strummed** with a pick, using **downstrokes** or **upstrokes**.

* Groups of related chords come together in **major** and **minor keys**, and each key is named after its 'home' chord. You've just learned the basic (**'three-chord trick plus one'**) harmonies for G, C, D and A majors, and A, E, B and F# minors.

* The **barré**, a technique allowing you to fret two or more strings simultaneously with a single finger, is a vital ingredient of the 'shiftable' shapes that can form chords higher up the neck.

Chapter 3

Theory and Practice

As a budding guitarist, you need to develop your knowledge of how music works, and that means learning a little about the construction of chords and scales, the way in which beats combine to make bars, and other subjects that may initially seem unrelated to the expansion of your instrumental skills...though they will help you to keep time, and to choose the correct notes and harmonies when you play! This chapter begins the process by providing a basic guide to musical theory, and introduces you to two different systems of written notation, explaining how the dots, lines and numbers they use correspond to your finger positions and pick strokes. And alongside all this mind-stretching material is a more directly physical challenge – your first encounter with a demanding new left-hand technique, the great barré.

Musical Basics: Pitches and the Stave

We've seen how 'the dots' (as musicians sometimes describe notation) can be used to put rhythms down on paper; now let's find out how they deal with pitches and melodies.

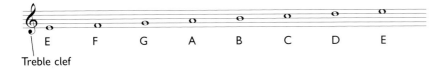

Treble clef — E   F   G   A   B   C   D   E

Left: The treble clef determines the placing of all these note pitches.

Each of the lines and spaces on the stave (see above) represents an individual note pitch. The position of the pitches is set by a symbol called a **clef**; guitar music uses a **treble** or **G clef**, which curls around the fourth line of the stave, indicating that it represents G. Normally, this would be the G with a frequency of 392Hz, seven semitones above middle C. However, to make the most commonly used notes in the centre of the guitar's range easier to read, its music is always written *an octave higher* than it actually sounds – so the 'G' line, with the clef curled around it, signifies the frequency of the guitar's 3rd string, which is tuned to the G at 196Hz. (It's only really important to remember this when you're playing with, or tuning to, other instruments.)

At the top of the next column is another stave, displaying the guitar's six open string pitches, plus a diagram linking the notes to their positions on the piano keyboard.

As you can see, the two lowest (E and A) strings don't fit onto the stave. To show their pitches, and those of other notes too low or

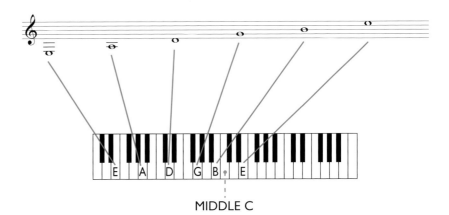

E   A   D   G   B   E

MIDDLE C

high to be accommodated on its five 'regular' lines, we use **ledger lines** – temporary extensions that work in exactly the same way as the permanent stave.

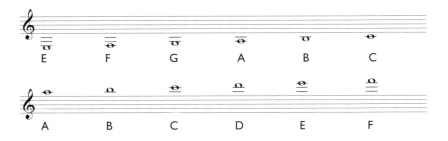

E   F   G   A   B   C

A   B   C   D   E   F

Above: Ledger-lined notes – a necessary evil when writing and reading musical notation.

There's another slight problem with our stave: its lines and spaces only have room for so-called **natural** notes (the 'white' keys on the piano). To write down a pitch such as F sharp (which is needed for chords like D major), we have to take an F, and prefix it with a # (sharp) symbol to indicate that its pitch should be *raised* by a semitone. To *lower* a natural note by the same amount, we use a **flat** (♭) sign. Any **accidental** (as these signs are termed) remains in force for a single bar before being automatically 'cancelled'; if a note has to be returned to its regular, unsharpened/unflattened pitch within a bar, this is done with a **natural** (♮) symbol (see diagram right).

Easing the learning curve

Try not to be too daunted by all these technicalities! It takes a while to get accustomed to notation, but persevering with it will pay huge dividends – boosting your ability to master new tunes and licks, and ultimately speeding up your development as a player. And, as we're about to see, 'the dots' becomes much easier to read when they're combined with **tablature** – another, simpler form of written music, which is explained overleaf.

Below: Following 'the dots': dividing your attention between the printed music and the guitar itself can take a little getting used to.

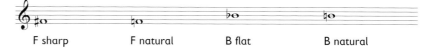

F sharp   F natural   B flat   B natural

Musical Basics: Tablature, Notation and Tunes

Unlike notation, tablature is specifically designed with guitarists in mind; instead of identifying particular notes and chords, it shows you where to find them on the fingerboard. It's written on six horizontal lines, each representing one of the instrument's strings. Superimposed onto these lines are numbers giving the left-hand fret positions needed to play the notes and chords of a song or piece; 0s indicate unfretted (open) strings, and if there's no number on a line, then the corresponding string stays silent.

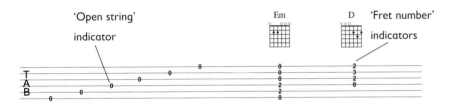

This section of tablature tells you to play the guitar's six open strings, one by one, from bottom E (6th) to the top E (1st).

Two familiar chords in 'tab' form: E minor, with the 4th and 5th strings held down at the 2nd fret (as shown by the numbers); and D major, with two silent bottom strings, an open 4th, and the top three strings held down at (respectively) the 2nd, 3rd and 2nd frets.

Tablature's relative simplicity makes it particularly popular with beginners, who may be put off by the apparent complexities of 'the dots'. However, it has a number of drawbacks: it doesn't display rhythms clearly, is difficult to read quickly, and is time-consuming to write without special computer software. Also, the fact that it's so closely tailored to the requirements of guitarists means that few other musicians can decipher it. However, because it displays actual fingerings, 'tab' is a great learning tool, and in this book, we'll be using it side by side with standard notation in all our musical examples from now on.

To help you get used to seeing tunes written out in notation and tablature, let's try playing a simple melody: the carol 'While Shepherds Watched Their Flocks By Night'. (This isn't exactly rock and roll...but as you're likely to know it well, you'll find it easy to spot any mistakes you may make while attempting to read it off the page.) We'll begin with a 'lower-register' version on the 5th, 4th and 3rd strings. Follow the numbers on the tablature to find the notes: those at the 2nd fret (on whichever string they occur) should be held down with your second finger, those at the 3rd fret with your third finger, and so on. (This may cause slight gaps when you have to fret consecutive notes on adjacent strings, like the C and F at the end of bar 1/start of bar 2; don't worry about these for now.) There are no first fret notes, so your index finger can have a brief rest; and your little finger will only be needed once – for the F# (indicated by the accidental) on the 4th fret/4th string at the end of the third bar (see diagram right).

We'll end by playing the same melody, an octave higher, on the guitar's top two strings. Use the same 'one digit per fret' left-hand fingering method as before (you'll need your index finger this time!), and all the notes should fall easily under your fingers, except perhaps the ledger-line A at the start of bar 5; see the photos and captions for help on how to reach for this. And as you practise the tune in its two registers, follow the rise and fall of the notes, and look closely at how they correspond to the position and movement of your hands on the instrument.

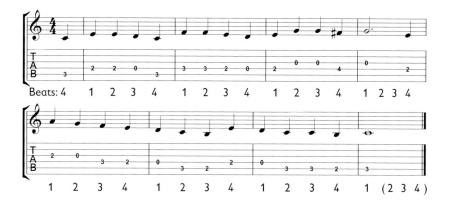

Above: All the exercises we've featured before have started on the first beat of a bar (often called the 'downbeat'). 'While Shepherds Watched…', though, begins on the less powerful 4th beat (an 'upbeat') – hence the single crotchet before the first bar line.

Below: Thanks to the open E at the end of bar 4, your little finger has time to stretch up to the 5th fret/5th string A at the start of bar 5.

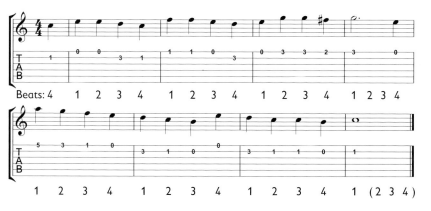

Above: The next note in bar 5, G, is held down with the second finger…

Right: …and the following F with the index.

53

Musical Basics: Chords and Key Signatures

One – admittedly simplistic – way to describe a chord is to call it 'a stack of notes'; and when you first see some of the harmonies you've recently learned written out on the stave, you may be taken aback by just how tall, and how daunting, they can appear. Here are three rather unsightly examples: a column of semibreves corresponding to our 'regular' six-string G major shape; and a pair of four-string chords, B major and F# major, both carrying essential, but ugly clusters of accidentals.

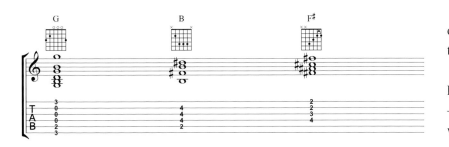

The notated G chord is harder to read, and less instantly recognizable, than the diagram above it. However, don't be too concerned: comparatively little printed guitar music includes fully written-out block chords of this kind. The multi-string shapes used for rhythm and accompaniment are much more likely to be signified by strumming marks (see earlier), symbols and letters, while notation and tab are largely reserved for solos and licks, which tend to contain fewer 'big' harmonies.

Thankfully, there is also a convenient way of reducing the number of accidentals needed when writing chords like those above. Individual keys use particular sharps and flats all the time (G major always requires an F#, D major has an F# and a C#, and so on), and their recurring accidentals can be collected together and placed at the start of each stave as **key signatures**. These serve as instructions to the performer to sharpen

or flatten all the indicated notes throughout the piece.

Below is a short chord sequence in D major – shown first without a key signature (but with the inevitable accidentals), and then with one, at the top of the following page.

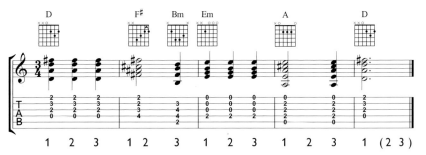

Left: The chord change in bar 2 here is musically effective, but hard to finger. To prevent squeaks and other unwanted noises, deaden the strings with your right hand just before you switch from F# to B minor (opposite above).

54

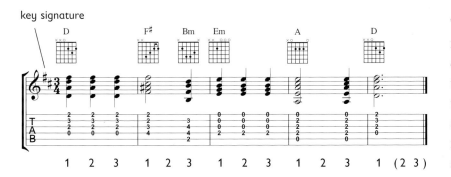

key signature

The second version is undoubtedly easier to read, and the presence of the key signature can also give you a 'tip-off' as to which key the piece is in – once you're able to recognize the different combinations of sharps and flats associated with all the various major and minors. We'll be studying keys and their key signatures in more detail later.

Taking chords a stage further

In the meantime, let's concentrate on chords – and the way certain selected notes from them can be used to create licks and figures, and even form the basis for fully-fledged lead guitar parts. Here's an easy, but quite effective example of a chordal figure, based on groups of notes from E minor, G and A. It also features bass notes, supplied by your open 5th string, which provide some rhythmical impetus while an A chord is left to ring above them. When you've mastered the exercise, you'll be ready for the more advanced licks on the next two pages.

Left: The transition from B minor to the E minor chord in bar 3 is much easier.

Below: This exercise includes two new harmonies: Em7 (the quavers using this chord in bar 3 should be played with a downstroke followed by an upstroke), and the shape without a name in bar 7. We'll be analyzing them later in the book; for now, just enjoy the effect they create!

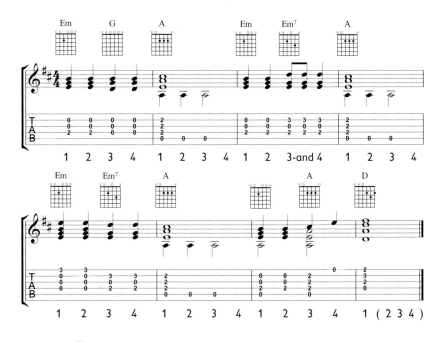

Licks and Figures-1

The lucky or inspired combination of sound, feel and context that makes some rock and pop guitar licks and motifs so special is impossible to define or quantify – but many of the 'building blocks' from which these phrases and figures are created are musically and technically quite straightforward.

In several cases, they're based on elementary, but satisfying adjustments to regular chords. Take a standard D, and add a G to it by fretting the first string with your little finger (see diagram); then release it (leaving the first string open) and strum again. You'll have heard both the harmonies (technically known as **suspended chords**) generated by these simple modifications on countless pop and rock records, usually in licks like the one shown here.

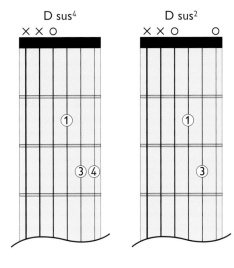

Left: Fingerings and names for the two 'suspended' harmonies described opposite, and used in the first two exercises.

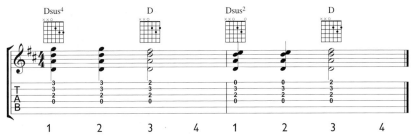

Syncopated rhythms

Played as written above, the lick may sound a bit staid and foursquare; you can spice it up by using what musicians call **syncopation**. This involves displacing some of the chords so that they don't always fall at the start of each beat. Try the next example, counting carefully as you do so. Because the final two chords in its second bar are **tied** together (see notation), you should pick only the first (quaver) note of the pair, and then let the strings ring on for the duration of the 'tied-on' minim (see diagram right).

The exercise opposite is also an old favourite, especially with bluesmen. It's in the key of E major, whose key signature automatically sharpens all Fs, Cs, Gs and Ds in the piece, unless otherwise indicated. Throughout its length (until the very end), the 6th and 5th strings provide a steady four-beat pulse. Above this is a riff starting with a 'wrong note' (A#) quaver that quickly moves up a semitone to B (another quaver, tied to a dotted minim; as before, pick just the first note, and then let the B ring until the end of the bar). The second bar contains a four-note 'walking' figure; see the photos and captions for how to finger and pick it, and watch out for the open-string D natural on its third beat.

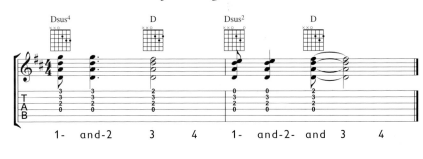

After completing the second bar, go back and play the opening two bars again, as indicated by the repeat signs on the stave (see notation below). Then move on to bars three and four, where the musical action shifts up to the 5th and 4th strings. Here, the first and tied notes are, respectively, D# and E, and the 'walking' notes are E, F#, and G natural: once again, beware of the accidental! The piece reverts to its original A#/B motif in the penultimate bar, before coming to rest on a bass E and B.

Below: The 'dotted' double bars surrounding the first two bars of this exercise are **repeat marks**; you should play everything within them twice.

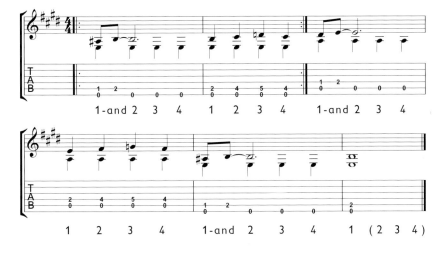

Above: We're now at bar 3 (after the repeat marks). Here, the index finger frets the D# quaver at the beginning of the bar, while the second finger hovers over the next note, E.

Left: Finger positions for the 'walking' riff in bar 2. As the index holds down the B at the 2nd fret/5th string, the third and fourth fingers are already in position above C# and D.

Right: 'Walking' on the 4th string to play E (2nd fret), F# (4th fret) and G (5th fret). The second finger keeps out of the way!

Licks and Figures-2

The figure you've just mastered could form the basis for an effective part if you were performing it entirely on your own, or accompanying a singer. However, with its constantly repeated notes, it has a fairly 'busy' feel, and might create too dense a texture if used in a band context, alongside (say) a bassist and drummer.

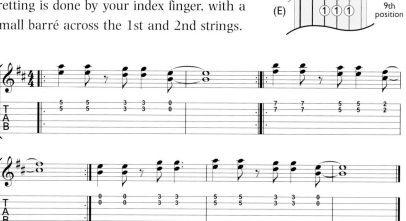

When working with other instruments, it's important to stay out of their way, and not to duplicate their roles. So, if you have drums – or even a drum machine – at your disposal, you should rely on them to spell out a song's basic rhythm, and allow your bass guitarist to provide its driving 'bottom end'. You'll then be free to supply melodic interest, embellish, and (where appropriate!) soar above the backing with your licks, figures and chords.

To do this effectively, you really need the power and sustain of an electric axe, and the exercises on these pages will sound best when played on one – though they're also well worth trying out on an acoustic. Those of you with electrics should select your back (bridge) pickup when practising them; they might also benefit from a touch of overdrive and distortion, if your amp can supply it, and the neighbours don't object!

The first lick we're going to try is simple, but packs quite a punch: its impact comes from its insistent syncopation, the bare-sounding interval (known to musicians as a **perfect 4th**) between its pairs of notes, and its use of the guitar's strident upper register. It also incorporates **rests** – strategically placed silences whose durations correspond to specific note lengths; see the panel opposite for a fuller explanation and list of these. The lick's first two phrases are played twice; strike the penultimate notes in the first, third, fifth

Right: Slide your index finger from the 2nd fret to the 5th, 7th, and 9th to create these three-note chords for the exercise opposite. 'Positions' are defined by the location of the index finger on the fretboard: when it's at the 2nd fret, your hand is said to be in the '2nd position'; at the 5th fret, it's in the '5th position', and so on.

and sixth bars with upstrokes, and everything else with downstrokes. As you can see from the adjacent photo, all the fretting is done by your index finger, with a small barré across the 1st and 2nd strings.

Left: The index finger at the 7th fret, forming the notes for the start of bar 3 in the first exercise.

Our second exercise is based on the 'standard' A shape (see diagram opposite), though here we refinger it with another small barré, and sound just the 2nd, 3rd and 4th strings. By sliding this shape from the 2nd fret up to the 5th, 7th and 9th positions, we can produce chords of A, C, D and E. For maximum effectiveness, keep your index finger pressed down on the neck while moving between them, and shift from fret to fret only a fraction of a beat before the next chord is 'due'. After cycling through all four harmonies, we combine them with a sequence of two-note figures (D-C#, F natural-E, G natural-F#, A-G#), played as 'pull-offs' with your second finger; see the photos and captions to learn how to do this.

'Pull-offs' (see photograph captions) are marked here with curved lines called **slurs**. Don't pick the second note in each slurred pair, which is sounded by the left hand.

Below: Fingering for the start of bar 3 in Exercise 2. As the index holds down a barré, the second finger frets D on the 3rd fret/2nd string, resulting in a suspended chord.

Below right: To produce a 'pull-off', the second finger releases its D with a slight 'flick'. This movement vibrates the string, which now sounds the note already held down by the index (in this case, C#) without the need for a plectrum stroke. The same technique is used for the other pull-offs in this exercise.

Above: The 2nd position barré needed for the A chord in Exercise 2.

RESTS

Music without occasional moments of silence would be dull and monotonous – and by inserting **rests** into notation, we can indicate exactly how long we want these breaks in sound to be, and show how they fit into the rhythmical scheme of a piece or song. As you can see from the chart below, each note has its own corresponding rest symbol. Rests can be dotted to extend their duration by half its 'regular' length, and are usually given the same amount of space on the stave as their equivalent notes, to make them easier to read and understand. There's one small

anomaly in the way the semibreve rest (shown in the first bar of the example) is used. Though it normally represents four beats, it's widely deployed in 2/4 and 3/4 to indicate a full bar of silence – despite the fact that bars in these time signatures are shorter than its specified duration.

Semibreve rest   Minim rest   Crotchet rest   Quaver rests

The Great Barré

The workout your index finger has been given in the last two exercises will stand it in good stead as we tackle the **great barré** – a major new left-hand skill whose mastery requires a certain amount of strength and persistence. You've already appreciated the importance of the small barré (the simultaneous fretting of two or three strings with just one digit) in giving you access to the upper reaches of the neck. The great barré is, quite literally, an extension of this technique; it involves a single-finger stretch across four or more strings, and is combined with other left-hand shapes to produce five- or six-string chords in a variety of keys and neck positions.

Below: A great barré at the 3rd fret position.

Let's begin by making a barré at the 3rd fret, where the strings are a little easier to hold down than they are nearer the nut. Lay your left-hand index finger across all six of them, brace behind the neck with your thumb (see photos), and press down firmly and evenly. Now strike the strings, and listen to the result. Musically, it's an uninteresting discord – but don't worry about that! Focus instead on how many of the strings are ringing out clearly. Do some of them start to buzz or become muffled as your finger weakens its grip? Have a few of them stayed completely dead because they aren't properly fretted? (The 5th and 4th can be particularly troublesome in this respect.) And last, but certainly not least, how well are your joints and muscles standing up to the considerable demands the barré is making on them? Release the chord after a few seconds, give your hand a rest, and then try again; identify incorrectly sounding strings with your pick, and, if necessary, help your index to fret them cleanly by supplying some temporary extra leverage from your second finger.

Once you're happy with the sound you're obtaining from the barré (getting it completely buzz-free may take a little time –

as always, be patient, and don't strain your finger), you'll be ready to transform the 'non-chord' it's currently providing into something harmonically useful. Hold your index across the neck as before (don't push the strings down with it yet), and position your third and fourth fingers at the 5th fret (two frets above the barré), on, respectively, the 5th and 4th strings. Now press your digits down, and strum: the result should be a six-string chord of G minor. You'll recognize the basic shape you've just created as a modified version of the old E minor chord you learned a little earlier; but now, thanks to the barré, you can move it around the neck, and play minor chords in all the positions your left hand can reach. On the next two pages, you'll be modifying other familiar fingerings and combining them with barrés, dramatically extending your repertoire of chords in the process.

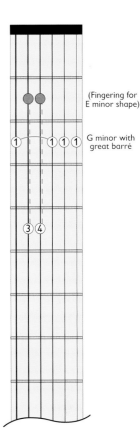

(Fingering for E minor shape)

G minor with great barré

Above: Position your thumb to give maximum support to your index finger.

Left: You used your second finger to reinforce your first small barrés; it can also help you hold down a great barré – until it's needed for other duties!

Above: A proper chord at last: a barréd 3rd position G minor.

Shifting Chords with the Barré

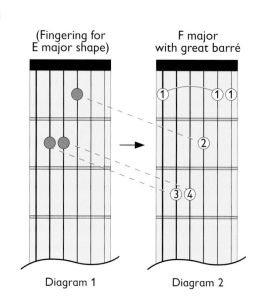

(Fingering for E major shape)

F major with great barré

Diagram 1   Diagram 2

Like the capo (see earlier), the great barré 'liberates' chord shapes whose dependence on open strings formerly confined them to the bottom of the neck. Almost every such fingering can be barréd; here, we show how this is done, and what the results can be.

We've already experimented with the 'E minor' shape: its close relative, E major, requires only one extra finger to produce a G# on the 3rd string (see diagram 1). Hold the note down with your second finger (not, for obvious reasons, the index we previously deployed for it), and use your third and fourth fingers on the other two fretted strings. Next, slide all three digits up a fret, making room for the index to form a great barré just behind them. We now have another moveable six-string chord: played in the first position, it's F major (see diagram 2 and photograph), and each subsequent single-fret shift raises its pitch by a semitone. Wherever it goes, however, the relative position of the notes in the harmonies it generates remains the same – as is the case with all shifted shapes. The bass root (F for F major, F# for F# major, etc.) is always on the 6th string, the major third (A for F major, A# for F# major, etc.) stays on the 3rd, and so on.

Let's go on to modify the standard 'A minor' and 'A major' shapes, in which the 6th string stays silent and the bass root is found on the 5th. Once again, as you can see from the photos and diagrams, a few refingerings are necessary; but when these have been accomplished, the newly barréd shapes can supply everything from Bb major and minor

(at the 1st position) to Ab major/minor at the 11th fret – if the shape of your guitar body allows you enough room to reach it...

Occasionally, though, the great barré can't help us to shift a chord, or the contortions it forces our fingers into are a little too awkward. Few guitarists bother to 'barré up' the basic 'G major' shape, as a fairly similar distribution of notes can be achieved far more easily via an 'E major'-type fingering. By contrast, the 'C major' shape can be moved along the neck quite easily – but a small barré is all that's needed to do so, as the illustrations demonstrate. A few performers find this chord too much of a stretch, and, like most of the other fingerings seen here, it does take some getting

Above: Barréd F major chord shape.

Below: Barréd Bb major chord shape.

(Fingering for A minor shape)

Bb minor with great barré
×

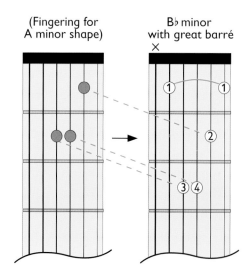

accustomed to. Nevertheless, it is unquestionably more comfortable than the four-string alternative pictured beside it – a chord that the author still finds exceptionally difficult after over thirty years of playing!

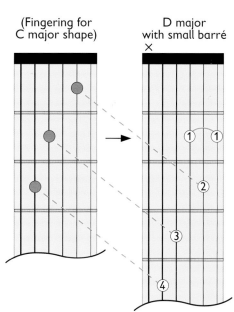

(Fingering for C major shape)

D major with small barré

Above: Small-barréd D major shape.

(Fingering for A major shape)

Bb major with great barré

(Fingering for D major shape)

Eb

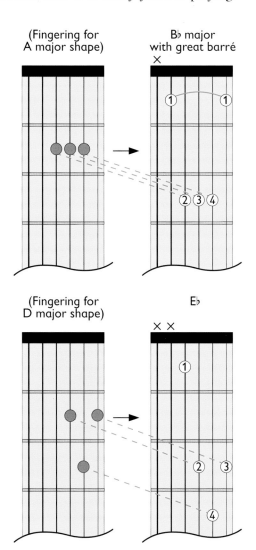

Left: Here, the shape shown in the diagram opposite forms a 3rd position F chord.

THE GUITAR'S 'GOOD' AND 'BAD' KEYS

Though the great barré gives us access to chords in an unlimited range of keys, there's no escaping the fact that playing for long periods in (say) Gb major or Bb minor is hard to manage on the guitar. The problem is less acute when soloing, as single notes in more 'remote' tonalities are no easier or harder to find than any others.

However, things are different when playing rhythm in keys that don't include open strings in their main chords. A, D, and E major are all favourites with guitarists, as most or all of their root notes can be produced without any fretting; but even 'three-chord tricks' in (say) Bb or Eb

demand constant barrés, and give no opportunity for the guitar's open strings to resonate freely, as they can in more 'friendly' keys.

Sometimes, you'll be free to pick your best keys, but more often, you'll have to 'grin and bear' these difficulties. If you're interested in jazz or swing, you'll usually be outnumbered by saxes and trumpets, which generally prefer 'flat' tonalities like the ones listed above; and when accompanying singers, you'll be obliged to play in the keys that best suit their vocal ranges. So, to maximize your musical versatility, keep practising those barrés!

The Barré in Action

In the dance-band era, when a guitarist's primary role was to pound out rhythm parts on a big-bodied acoustic while louder instruments like saxes and trumpets took the limelight, players had to use five- and six-string chords in order to be heard. For this reason, old-fashioned guitar tutors often devoted considerable space to exercises that featured long sequences of great barréd shapes – trying the patience as well as the muscles of many of their readers in the process!

The great barré remains an essential technique, but the dense textures it can generate aren't always appropriate to modern musical styles. Multi-note chords like the ones you've been learning are sometimes abbreviated to two- or three-string shapes that may only 'hint' at the harmonic content of their originals; they can also be punctuated or linked together with licks and other figures to provide variety and interest. Examples of these 'tricks of the trade' are found in the examples below, which demonstrate some of the ways in which the barré can be used to add flexibility and fluency to your playing.

The first exercise starts with a sequence of heavy chords, takes you up the neck for some four-string shapes (try picking these a little more gently), then moves down again, via a tricky transition from E minor to C in bar 5, to a ringing conclusion. Make sure that the open 5th string in the penultimate bar is struck only on the first and third beats, and left to vibrate; and pick the quavers in this bar, as well as those in bars 1, 3 and 5, with down- and upstrokes.

Cutting down on chord grids

Wherever appropriate, the notation in this chapter has included chord diagrams to guide you; but these are probably superfluous now you're more accustomed to 'dots' and tab, so we won't always be showing them in future. The notes and shapes in Exercise Two shouldn't prove too difficult to decipher, although its final two bars contain some easily fingered but more 'exotic' suspended harmonies, similar to those that appeared a little earlier. Enjoy the effect they create – soon, we'll be looking more closely at how they're constructed.

Below left: Don't be alarmed by the excursions up the fretboard required by Exercise Two – their fingerings are all familiar. The top left picture shows the 5th position small barré for the A minor chords in bar 1 (i.e. the first full bar after the upbeat crotchet).

Below: A bar later, the index moves down two frets to play G and D on the top two strings, while the second finger completes the chord with a B on the 4th fret/3rd string.

Above: The three-note C major chord in bar 3 uses the same fingerings as the one in the previous photograph, shifted up to the 8th position.

Above: This is the B minor chord for bar 4 – a straightforward small barré across the 1st, 2nd and 3rd strings at the 7th fret. After you've struck it, get ready to play the bass E on the open 6th string!

What You've Learned

* Standard musical **notation** uses a five-line **stave**. The notes appearing on it show which pitches should be sounded; their durations are indicated by their look and shape, and by their stems and tails (if any).

* **Tablature** ('tab'), a six-line, guitar-based alternative to notation, shows which strings and fret positions are needed to play a piece's notes and chords.

* Vertical lines on the stave or tab mark out **bars** – rhythmical patterns of strong and weak beats, usually based around **crotchet**, **minim** or **quaver** note-lengths.

* The number of beats in a bar, and their type (crotchet, minim, quaver etc.) are defined by the two-figure **time signature** displayed at the start of a notated piece of music.

* Note lengths can be modified by **dots** and **ties**. Placing a dot after a note lengthens it by half its original duration; tied notes are struck just once, and held for the total number of their combined beats.

* Note pitches can be temporarily altered by **accidentals** (sharps, flats and naturals). When placed before a note, a sharp raises it by a semitone, a flat lowers it by the same amount, and a natural 'cancels' any earlier sharps and flats. Accidentals apply only within the bar where they occur.

* To raise or lower particular notes throughout a piece of music, a **key signature** is used. This appears at the start of every stave, and indicates the sharps and flats required for the major or minor key that the piece is 'in'.

Chapter 4
Scales and Beyond

On the next few pages, we continue our exploration of the building blocks of music, progressing from 'do-re-mi' to tonics, subdominants and dominants, revealing the mysteries of the melodic and harmonic minor scale ... and discovering how understanding such terms and concepts can speed up and systemize your study of the guitar. We also examine the underlying architecture of a range of common chords – some already familiar, others offering new exciting new tonal colours. Among the second group is the so-called 'dominant 7th', whose prosaic name does little to convey its almost endless versatility, or the vital role it plays throughout pop and jazz. The major- and minor-key exercises towards the end of the chapter demonstrate some of its special attributes and flavours.

Your First Scale

Scales...their very mention provokes gloom in the hearts of countless former piano students, who associate them with hours of tedious practice, and the threat of a rap over the knuckles from teacher as punishment for a misplaced finger. On the piano, scales are dreary, monotonous, and (perhaps worst of all) predictable. Because the clear, logical layout of the keyboard makes finding their constituent notes relatively straightforward, learning them brings little sense of adventure or achievement; while being made to repeat them ad nauseam can quickly dull the enthusiasm of even the keenest player.

For guitarists, scales have more practical value. Practising them helps you develop a mental 'map' of the fretboard (essential on an instrument with no black and white keys to guide your left hand), and provides you with patterns of fingerings that allow you to locate any note you need, wherever it lies on the neck. Acquiring this knowledge takes time, but the learning process will feel more like a voyage of discovery than a chore, as you realize that each new scale can unlock a little more of the guitar's potential, and reveal fresh possibilities for tunes and riffs.

We'll begin our exploration of scales at the bottom end of the neck – 'a very good place to start' (as Julie Andrews puts it in *The Sound of Music*) because of the large number of different scales it's possible to find there. First, let's get used to fretting successions of single notes by trying out a two-octave **chromatic** scale – something that sounds very different to the regular eight-step major featured in Julie's famous song 'Do-Re-Mi', as it moves in semitone steps, and takes in every note in its path. Prepare to play it by placing your left-hand fingers above the instrument's first four fret positions on the 6th string, as shown in photograph 1. Now

strike the open E string, followed in turn by the four notes (F, F#, G, G#) that lie beneath your fingers (see notation). Pause for a moment, lift your little finger clear of the 4th fret, and regroup your digits over the 5th string (see photograph 2). When you're ready, pick the open A, and then strike the next four notes using the same sequence of fingers. We use almost exactly the same technique for the rest of the scale; the only deviation occurs at the 3rd string, where, due to the way the guitar is tuned, only three fretted notes are required before we move up to the open 2nd (see photograph 3).

This symbol is a 'pause' sign; it's an instruction to extend the length of a note or rest for as long as you feel is appropriate.

SCALES GALORE...

Just how many scales are there? It's an almost impossible calculation – but taking in major, minor, pentatonic, modal, whole-tone, 'enigmatic', and non-European examples, the total must run into many thousands.

The largest compendium of them ever published was Russian-born, US-based academic and composer Nicholas Slonimsky's 244-page *Thesaurus of Scales and Melodic Patterns*, which appeared in 1947 and is still selling well.

In-depth study of scales might seem alien to the freewheeling spirit of rock and roll…but a considerable number of star performers find them a technically rewarding, and even liberating part of their rehearsal routine. King Crimson frontman Robert Fripp once commented to *Guitar Player* magazine that he enjoyed 'practising all different keys and scales and becoming familiar with them, and then…walk[ing] on stage, completely forgetting all [I'd] ever practised, and just *being*.'

Left – Photograph 2: The one-fret-per-finger technique is applied to the 5th string.

Below – Photograph 3: Because of the smaller interval between the 3rd and 2nd strings, the next note after the B♭ being held down here on the 3rd will be an unfretted B natural from the 2nd.

Above – Photograph 1: Four frets, four fingers – getting ready to play the chromatic scale notes on the 6th string.

A stream of semitones

Once you've played the scale slowly, with gaps at each string change, see if you can manage it more fluently, as a steady, unbroken line of quavers. You'll find this easier to do if you hold your fingers as close to the fingerboard as possible, reducing their vertical movement to a minimum.

Major Scales-1

To reach the notes for the chromatic scale you've just played, you assigned consecutive fret positions – in this case, the first four frets – to adjacent left-hand fingers (the 1st, 2nd, 3rd and 4th), and made each finger responsible for all the notes found at its 'own' fret, on whichever string they occurred. The 'one-fret-per-finger' technique is crucial to scale playing on the guitar, and in a moment, we'll be applying it to the most commonly used scale in all Western music – the **major**.

You've already encountered major keys and the 'three-chord tricks' associated with them, and played a major-key tune ('While Shepherds Watched Their Flocks By Night' – see earlier). You'll also be familiar with the song 'Do-Re-Mi' from *The Sound of Music*, which we mentioned on the last two pages, and whose melody and lyrics helpfully set out the major's 'ingredient' notes – from 'Do' back to 'Do'. Let's now take a closer look at how the scale is constructed.

Thanks to Richard Rodgers and Oscar Hammerstein, we know that the major consists of eight notes, counting the starting note (**keynote**) twice. The keynote can be any of the 12 notes in the chromatic scale, but whichever is chosen, the major always follows this pattern:

Its second note is two semitones (= one tone) above the keynote;
Its third note is one tone above the second note;
Its fourth is a semitone above its third;
Its fifth is a tone above its fourth;
Its sixth is a tone above its fifth;
Its seventh is a tone above its sixth;
Its octave keynote is a semitone above its seventh.

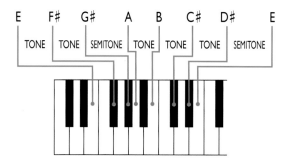

Here's a piano-style diagram demonstrating how the 'formula' explained above applies to a specific major scale – E major. Having seen its intervals set out on the keyboard, let's now locate them on the guitar neck as we prepare to play a two-octave scale of E. Position your left-hand fingers above the 6th string (as you did for the chromatic scale), start by picking the open bass E, and then follow the notation and tablature to find the other notes. Remember to hold down the ones at the first fret position with your first finger, those at the second fret with your second finger, and so on.

Left: The only notes required from the 3rd string in our scale of E are G# (1st fret), which has just been played, and the A at the 2nd fret – being held down here by the second finger.

Above: Near the start of the E major scale: as the second finger frets F# on the 2nd fret/6th string, the little finger prepares to play G# at the 4th fret.

Left: In this picture, we've almost reached the top of the E scale's second octave. The second finger frets C# (2nd fret/2nd string) while the fourth heads for D# (4th fret/2nd string).

Above: The transition from C# (4th fret/5th string) to D# (1st fret/4th string).

Several other two-octave majors fall just as easily under the fingers on this section of the fretboard; try the G major and A♭ major scales shown below – and once you've mastered playing them in ascending motion, as notated here, see if you can manage them in the opposite direction!

The unfamiliar key signature of A♭ major, indicating that all Bs, Es, As and Ds in the scale should be flattened.

Major Scales-2

The guitar's open strings, which are so useful when combined with simple shapes to generate basic chords in the guitar's 'good keys' (see previous feature box), can also help us to play numerous one-octave major scales. Here are two short exercises in the keys of C and D major, using 'three-chord trick' harmonies combined with scale passages.

While practising them, you'll find that you scarcely have to move your left hand from its chord-fretting positions to locate the scale notes, which can often be produced merely by lifting or replacing the occasional finger.

We can experiment with these by taking part of the tune from the C major exercise you've just tried, and transposing it up an octave.

In its original version, the 'jump' from C to C posed no problems, as both notes were part of the familiar first-position C major chord shape. Now, though, you need to get quickly from the lower C, previously supplied from the 1st fret on the 2nd string, to the one an octave above it, which can only be found at the 8th fret on the 1st string. The resultant leap is much too awkward to be practicable –

The limiting factor with the scales shown above, and with those on the previous few pages, is their restricted range. When you keep your left hand over the first four frets, the highest note available, using the 'one-fret-per-finger' rule, is the Ab at the 4th fret of the 1st string. In order to stretch beyond it, and to play a greater number of two-octave scales, it's necessary to move further up the neck, and to master some new left-hand techniques.

Right: Even the biggest hand can't reach the C an octave above the one being fretted here on the 2nd string!

74

but what if you placed your second finger at the 8th fret, 'covering' the neighbouring frets with your other fingers, and played the passage like this (right)?

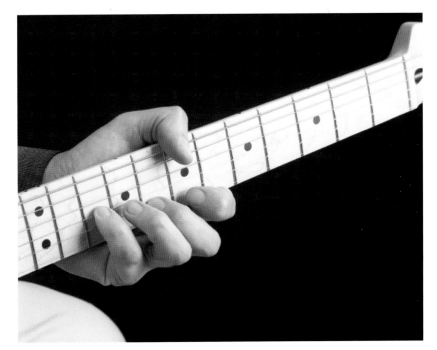

Above: Fingerings for the start of the exercise above: the little finger holds down a C at the 10th fret/4th string, with the second finger ready at the octave C (8th fret/1st string).

Right: The descending G, F and E in bar two of the exercise: the G comes from the 8th fret/2nd string, and is taken by the second finger, while the fourth and third fingers prepare to play F and E at, respectively, the 10th and 9th frets on the 3rd string.

There's no difficulty now, as all the notes are within the span of your left hand; and if you wanted to extend the scale downwards (as shown below), you could do so without the need for any extra wrist or arm movement.

On the next two pages, we'll find out how to use this fingering for major scales in other keys – and examine some alternative ways of approaching them.

Major Scales-3

The fingerings you've just learned provide a two-octave scale not just in C, but for major keys from F# (for which you'd start at the 2nd fret of the 6th string) up to D (beginning from its 10th fret). They may be impossible to manage in higher positions if you're playing a guitar with only 12 frets clear of its body and/or no cutaway, like the one in the photo; but on some electrics, you should be able to continue using the scale even beyond the 12th fret.

This 'universal' diagram summarizes the string and finger placings required to produce these scales, and is valid for all reachable keys.

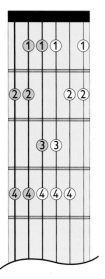

Left: By starting your ascending major scale on the 6th string – holding down its first note with your second finger, and then following the illustrated finger positions upwards (2nd scale note = fourth finger/6th string, 3rd scale note = first finger/ 5th string, 4th scale note = second finger/5th string, and so on), you can play majors in a wide range of keys, as explained above.

Thanks to the 'one-fret-per-finger' method, all eight notes are easily accessible; but after you've arrived at the D on the 3rd string (currently fretted with your little finger), there seem to be no available digits to continue upwards. The solution is to make a rapid shift in position: after holding down the C# on the 3rd string with your third finger, move your index up to the D on the next fret, and play the upper octave as indicated below:

Position shift here

Below: As usual, each left-hand finger is 'responsible' for a specific fret here: 4th fret notes are taken by the index, 5th fret ones by the second, etc.

Above: The fingerings for the first octave of the scale are identical to those in the preceding example. At the 'shift' point, your left hand moves from the 4th position (as explained earlier, 'positions' are defined by the placing of the index finger on a specific fret) to the 7th position – with your index playing all subsequent 7th fret notes (like the D at the start of the second octave of our scale), your second finger covering the 8th fret, and so on.

Let's now explore another two-octave major scale 'route' up the fretboard. It starts from the 5th string, held down by the second finger, and we'll try it first in the key of D. Here's the first octave.

Left: Commencing the second octave of the D major scale: the index holds down the D at the 7th fret/3rd string, while the third finger prepares to play E at the 9th fret.

Above: The third finger plays C# at the 6th fret/3rd string, with the index finger poised for its leap upwards to the start of the second octave.

Left: We've now reached the top three notes of the scale, which all come from the 1st string; the index plays B (7th fret), and the following C# and D are covered by the third and fourth fingers at the 9th and 10th frets.

The 'leap' in the middle of this scale means that it can only be used for about six major keys – B (starting at the 2nd fret) to E (starting at the 7th fret) – before it runs out of neck space. However, it's useful, and well worth adding to your repertoire. This diagram will remind you how it works.

Right: The starting point for the first octave of this scale pattern is the 5th string, with the first note fretted by the second finger. The shift in position (third finger/3rd string to first finger/3rd string) always occurs at the beginning of the second octave.

Position shift here

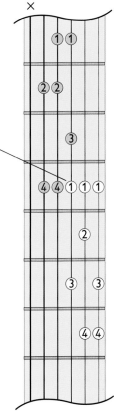

KEEPING YOUR FINGERS IN POSITION

When first attempting scales or other single-note passages, many guitarists tend to lift their left hand fingers several centimetres clear of the fingerboard after fretting a note, and 'come down' onto the strings from a similarly excessive distance. This isn't a problem when practising slowly; but if it becomes a habit, it will severely restrict your ability to execute fast successions of notes, as you waste time and energy moving your digits through dead air. Try and minimize the gap between each finger and the strings. Don't allow your fingertips to flatten as they press down on the frets; and do your best to make all your left hand movements as economical as possible.

Minor Scales-1

Minor scales are a little more complex than their major counterparts, as the term 'minor' is used to describe two different (though closely related) sequences of notes. As we've already discovered, the minor's defining factor is the presence of a three-semitone interval (known as a minor third) between the keynote and third in its 'root' chord; let's now look at the intervals separating the first five notes of its scale.

The minor's second note is one tone above the keynote;

Its third note is a semitone above the second note;

Its fourth is a tone above its third;

Its fifth is a tone above its fourth.

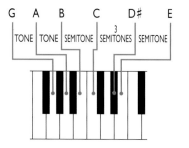

Left: The second part of an E harmonic minor scale as it appears on the keyboard

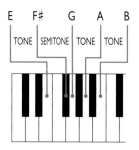

Above: Here's the start of a scale of E minor, set out on a piano keyboard to illustrate the gaps between its first five steps.

So far, things are fairly clear; but the distances between the remaining intervals depend on whether the minor scale we're dealing with is what musicians refer to as a **melodic** or a **harmonic** minor. The harmonic minor is simpler, but less commonly used: its sixth note is a semitone above its fifth, while its seventh note lies a **minor third** (three semitones) above its sixth. After this curiously placed interval, which gives the scale an almost oriental flavour, there's a more normal semitone between the seventh and the octave keynote.

Melodic minors sound more conventionally 'Western', but have an unusual feature of their own – their notes change, depending on whether the scale is rising or falling. On its ascent, the melodic has tones between its fifth and sixth, and its sixth and seventh; a semitone separates the seventh and the octave keynote. Going down, the intervals work as follows:

The seventh is one tone below the octave keynote;

The sixth is one tone below the seventh;

The fifth is a semitone below the sixth;

The remaining intervals are the same as for the rising scale.

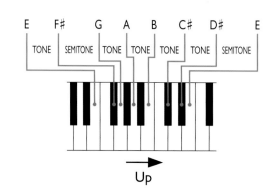

Left: E melodic minor in its ascending form.

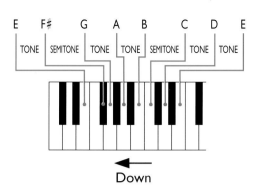

Above: E melodic minor in its descending form.

Thankfully, both the harmonic and melodic minors are easier (and rather more fun) to play on the guitar than they are to describe! Let's begin, as we did with the majors, by learning some two-octave versions of both types, using as many open strings as possible. Here are two pairs of E minor and G minor scales; both should be fingered using the 'one-finger-per-fret' method, with the index assigned to the 1st fret, the second finger to the 2nd fret, and so on.

E minor (harmonic)

E minor (melodic)

G minor (harmonic)

Key signature of G minor: Bs and Es are flattened – except where altered by accidentals

G minor (melodic)

Left: Knowledge of scales helps you create licks and solos, and makes it easier to find the notes you need.

Minor Scales-2

The harmonic minor scale appears only rarely in Western pop, though it features strongly in Spanish flamenco and other ethnic music, and is also widely used by classical composers. Here's a simple exercise in the key of D minor that gives some idea of its possibilities.

Key signature of D minor

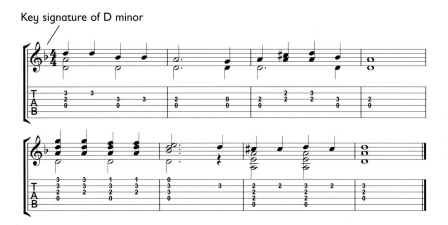

Left: As this piece is in D minor, the 'active ingredients' of its harmonic minor scale are B♭ and C#: listen to the distinctive effect they create. It's based around chord shapes (like D minor and A) that you're already familiar with, and you don't need to stray beyond the first three frets to play it – so you should be able to work out suitable left-hand fingerings without too much difficulty!

In contrast, the melodic minor forms the basis for thousands of songs and tunes. Let's try one of the most familiar of them, *Greensleeves*, in A minor (see right).

As you can see, the choice of sharpened or flattened 6th and 7th notes (F/F# and G/G#) is often – but not always – determined by whether the tune is moving upwards or downwards; and at the start of its second section, *Greensleeves* departs even further from the 'official' notes of the scale by following a G natural with an F#. There are a number of explanations for such deviations (mostly based on arcane technicalities), but their best justification is simply that they sound good – and that, as a famous composer once remarked, when it comes to making music, 'the rules should be our humble servants'.

The need to reach some of these 'unexpected' notes means that we have to make occasional adaptations and modifications of our own when using

New time signature –
see panel

Semiquaver –
see panel

'1st-' and '2nd-time'
bars – see panel

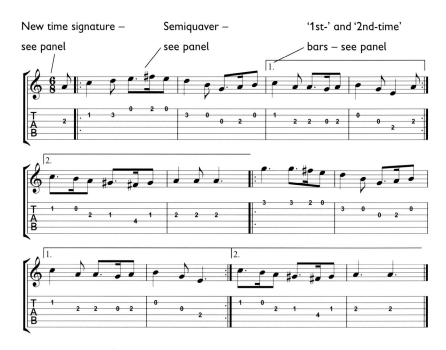

standard minor-key fingerings – few of which, even in their 'regular' forms, are quite as straightforward as their major counterparts. The useful two-octave melodic minor fingering at the top of the next page requires two left-hand leaps as it progresses up and down the fretboard. It begins on the 5th string with a note held down by the

Above: All the notes for *Greensleeves* come either from open strings, or from first position fingerings (index finger on 1st fret, second finger on 2nd fret etc.)

index finger, and can work in keys between Bb minor (starting at the 1st fret) and D minor (starting at the 5th fret), and can possibly be taken higher, depending on your instrument. We'll try it in B minor; follow the notation (right), finger placings and photos below to play it.

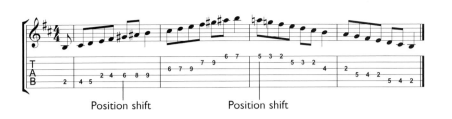

Position shift   Position shift

Left: The first two pictures illustrate the position shift between the 5th and 6th steps of the ascending B melodic minor scale (see text). Here, the third finger holds down F# on the 4th fret/4th string as the index prepares to move upwards.

After starting on B (index finger, 2nd fret/5th string) and sounding the first five notes of the scale on the 5th and 4th strings using the 'one-fret-per-digit' method, shift your index to the G# at the 6th fret on the 4th string; this will bring the remaining upward notes under your fingers. Once you've got to the top B (7th fret, 1st string, second finger), move your wrist down two frets and place your little finger on the 1st string A (5th fret). You can now reach all the subsequent descending notes without any further position shifts.

Below: The other position shift in B melodic minor: the little finger has just moved from the 7th fret/1st string (where it had been playing B) to A natural at the 5th fret/1st string. G natural, F#, and the rest of the downward sequence of notes in the scale are all easily accessible.

Left: The index has now completed its 'jump' to the 6th fret/4th string, and is playing G# while the third and fourth fingers hover over A# and B.

6/8 TIME, SEMIQUAVERS, AND FIRST- AND SECOND-TIME BARS

The notation for *Greensleeves* shown opposite contains three unfamiliar features. Its 6/8 time signature indicates that there are 6 'eighth-notes' (i.e. quavers, each 'worth' one-eighth of a semibreve) per bar. However, these are grouped into pairs of dotted crotchets, giving a '2-beat' feel to the music. Counting '1-2-3 2-2-3' will help you to place individual quavers within the overall pulse.

The 'doubletailed' notes following the dotted quavers are **semiquavers**, whose duration is half that of a quaver. The distinctive dotted-quaver/semiquaver/quaver pattern in

Greensleeves can be counted out as '1-2-and-3' (dividing the second quaver in half), with the dotted quaver falling on the '1', the semiquaver on the 'and', and the final quaver on '3'.

Finally, *Greensleeves*' two repeated sections incorporate bars bracketed '1' and '2'. The first time you perform each half of the tune, you should include the '1' (a.k.a. 'first time') bars and omit those marked '2'. On the repeat, ignore the 'first time' bars and, after playing the bar before the brackets, jump to the section marked '2'.

Minor Scales-3

Here's a summary of the fingerings for our two-octave melodic minor in diagram form.

Right: In this fingering, the ascending melodic minor starts with the keynote being fretted by the index finger on the 5th string. The shift in position (3rd finger/4th string to first finger/4th string – see diagram) occurs between the 5th and 6th steps of its first octave.

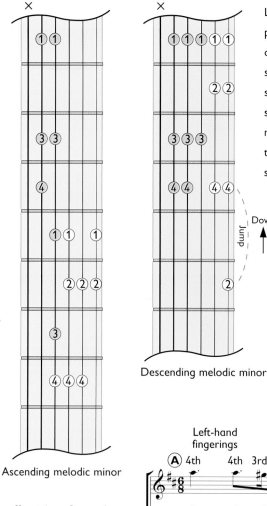

Ascending melodic minor

Descending melodic minor

Down

Jump

Left: Going down, the position shift takes place just after the top note of the scale, which is played by the second finger on the 1st string. The descending 7th note is then held down by the fourth finger, on the same string two frets below.

Above – photograph 1: Playing the A, G# (held down here by the third finger) and F# on the 1st string in Section A of the *Greensleeves* extracts.

Patterns like these are excellent 'roadmaps' to the neck – but in the real musical world, where minor-key tunes don't always have their sharpened and flattened 6th and 7ths in the order prescribed by the scale, it's often necessary to make a few 'detours' from the standard fingerings. Let's say, for example, that you wanted to play *Greensleeves* not in A minor (as it appeared on the previous two pages), but in B minor. On the right are three sections of the song written out in (or, to use the technical term, transposed into) the new key.

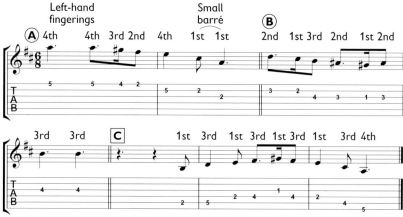

Though the fingerings shown above the notes in these transposed extracts are based on those for the regular melodic minor scale, they've had to be adjusted to accommodate the G#s in Sections A and B (a descending melodic minor would have G naturals here).

Far left – photograph 2:
Greensleeves Section B –
the second finger holds
down A# on the 3rd
string while the index
moves back to play G#.

Left – photograph 3:
The fourth and fifth
notes (F# and G#) of
Greensleeves Section C.

In Section A, the change is minimal, as the third finger is readily available to hold down the 'unexpected' note (see photograph 1). However, the lower-register G# in Section 2 would be unreachable with standard scale fingerings – unless you. break the 'one-finger-per-fret' rule by stretching your index finger back to the 1st fret on the 3rd string, as shown in photograph 2. The snag in Section C (the start of the tune, 'shifted' to the lower octave) has nothing to do with the sharpened or flattened 6ths and 7ths – here, the unplayability is caused by the leap up to G# on the 4th string, which disrupts the flow of the tune. Once again, the index finger can come to the rescue, supplying this note from the 1st fret on the 3rd string (see photograph 3).

A similar stretch is needed if we want to produce a harmonic minor scale from this pattern. By starting from the 5th string with the first finger, as before, all the necessary notes can be found without repositioning the left hand – but after getting to G at the 3rd fret on the 1st string, you'll need to extend your third finger to the 6th fret for A# before holding down the top B, a fret above it, with your little finger.

Right – photograph 4: The third finger
stretches out to A# (6th fret/1st string) at
the top of the harmonic minor pattern.

Here's the full scale in notation and as a diagram.

Scales form a vital part of guitar playing, and on the last few pages, we've only begun to explore the many methods of fingering them. However, having learned a little about their structure, it's now time for us to take a closer look at their relationship with chords – and to expand our knowledge of harmony in the process.

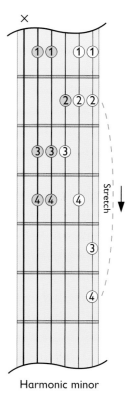

Harmonic minor

Above: The notes and
fingerings for the
harmonic minor scale
remain the same in both
directions.

Scales and New Chords-1

So far, we've confined ourselves almost exclusively to elementary 'three-chord trick plus one' harmonies. The rest of this chapter goes beyond the basics by focusing on the individual 'steps' of the major and minor scales, demonstrating how they relate to one another, and using them as 'building blocks' for richer, more imaginative chords.

By now, you'll have no difficulty in identifying the individual notes (C, D, E etc.) of the C major scale shown below. However, musicians sometimes use other, more generalized terms for the steps (or **degrees**) of major and minor scales. They include numbers, short, easily memorable names (Do, Re, Mi, etc.), and the more formal titles also listed below. Like letters in algebra, such terms make it possible to discuss notes and chords, and their function and place in the scale, without constantly referring to specific keys.

Music, but originally part of a system called 'tonic solfa', designed for singers who couldn't read standard notation) isn't used by guitarists; and only three of the more technical names for the scale steps – **tonic**, **subdominant**, and **dominant** – are widely heard outside the confines of classical music.

So, relating this new nomenclature to the basic chords in the key of C major:
The **tonic** is, of course, the **root** chord (C major itself) in our 'three-chord trick';
the other two basic C major chords (F and G) are, respectively, the **subdominant** and **dominant**;

The **relative minor** of C major is A minor (the minor chord from the 6th or **submediant** note of the major scale).

Above: Starting young…though reduced-size instruments are available, children should switch to 'regular' guitars (like the one seen here) as soon as they can manage them.

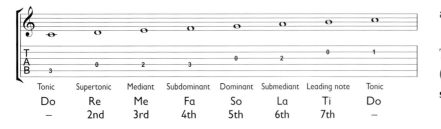

Tonic	Supertonic	Mediant	Subdominant	Dominant	Submediant	Leading note	Tonic
Do	Re	Me	Fa	So	La	Ti	Do
–	2nd	3rd	4th	5th	6th	7th	–

Note: We're using C major for this and our next few examples – but remember that the terms and numbers seen here apply to *all other keys* as well.)

These are the most common ways of describing the notes of the scale – but you don't need to learn them all! 'Do-Re-Mi' terminology (familiar from *The Sound of*

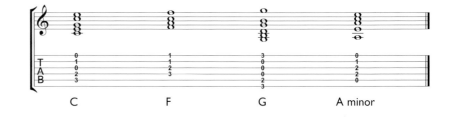

C	F	G	A minor

Let's now use some of these names and numbers to define and describe a few 'spiced-up' harmonies. Our tonic (C major) chord already comprises the 1st, 3rd and 5th degrees of the scale (C, E and G): what would happen if we combined it with each of the four remaining notes – the **2nd** (D), **4th** (F), **6th** (A), or **7th** (B)? Logically enough, adding a 6th creates an **added 6th** chord (**C6 or C add 6** – its fingering is shown in the photograph on the next page). And you've already encountered harmonies that temporarily replace the 3rd with the 2nd and 4th, resulting in so-called **suspended**

chords like the **C sus2** and **C sus4** shown below, both of which seem naturally to lead back (or **resolve**) to the tonic.

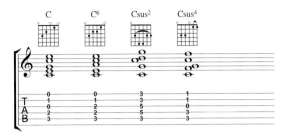

However, what happens when we add a 7th to a major chord is a little more complex, and we'll examine it further overleaf.

Below: Many popular songs, especially early Beatles numbers, use added 6th chords (these players are holding down two versions of an A6), and suspensions.

Scales and New Chords-2

The unique sound and 'feel' provided by 7th chords gives them a very special place in music, and particularly in pop, jazz and blues. There are two distinct types of 7th in any scale. The first one we're going to consider is the **leading note** (see previous pages), which lies a semitone below the octave keynote, and 11 semitones – an interval termed a **major 7th** – above the root keynote.

Below: The C6 shape, which can also be shifted up the neck to play 6th chords in other keys.

Major 7th

Above: The major 7th interval from C to B. Obviously, major 7ths exist between any two notes separated by 11 semitones (D and C#, E♭ and D, etc.)

Above: Here's the same major 7th interval in notation and tablature.

The major 7th clashes slightly with the keynote – but by retaining the bass root (C in our C major example) and removing the uppermost C from the chord, we produce a piquant new harmony (**C maj 7**) that works particularly well in sequence with regular C major and **C6** chords.

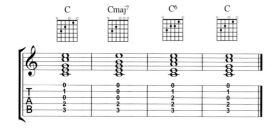

Left: To play 'C maj 7', simply lift your index finger off the 2nd string C used in the preceding 'C' shape. 'C6', as shown in the photograph above, is a little trickier: its root C (3rd fret/5th string) is held down by the fourth; its E (2nd fret/4th string) by the second finger; the A on the 2nd fret/3rd string by the third; and the 1st fret/2nd string C by the index.

The other, even more extensively used 7th interval is the minor 7th, just a semitone narrower than its major counterpart (it's separated by ten semitones from the root note).

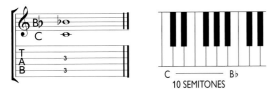

Minor 7th

When incorporated into a 'straight' major chord, the minor 7th creates a harmony known as a **dominant 7th** – so called because it's widely used as a colourful alternative to the standard dominant chord in both major and minor keys. 'Dom 7s' can propel a song or tune inexorably 'homewards' towards their associated tonics, and this effect makes them important 'building-blocks' in nearly all styles of jazz, pop and classical music.

To get the feel of these crucial chords, try out the dominant 7th-tonic progressions shown below. As 'dom 7s' differ from regular dominants by only one note, you should find their shapes easy to master; more detailed fingering diagrams for them can be found in the Chord Directory at the end of the book.

'Dom 7s', and the blues'

The dominant 7th has many other possibilities and applications. Its tendency to resolve to the chord a fifth below it means that it can act as a musical pathway, leading a piece into regions far removed from its original keynote. If, for instance, you played the C7 to F progression at the start of our previous example, but chose to continue via F7 to B♭7, and then to E♭7, A♭7 and so on, you would eventually pass through the dominant 7ths for all 12 notes of the chromatic scale – and, after encountering D7 and G7, arrive back at C7, where you started! (This so-called 'cycle of fifths' is one of the features that underpins the system of keys and harmonies used in Western music.) Of more immediate interest to most guitarists, though, is the 'dom 7's' role in blues and jazz. The flattened interval at its heart is a vital element in these genres, and in the mainstream pop styles that borrow from them; we'll be savouring its distinctive flavour in several forthcoming exercises.

Below: The chord diagrams here use the standard abbreviations (C7, D7 etc.) for dominant 7ths. Most of the 'dom 7' shapes are closely derived from those for standard major chords; the adjacent photo demonstrates the fingering for C7.

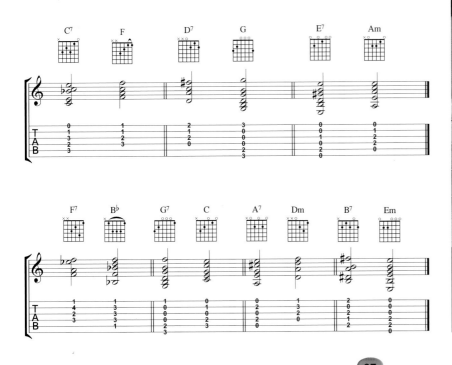

Exercises Using 6ths and 7ths

The first of the four short exercises here is in D major, and uses a pair of chords (D sus 2 and D sus 4) that you have already encountered. It also features Em 7 and A7 (the dominant 7th chords of D major's second and fifth degrees), and includes an unfamiliar harmony (Em add 9) in its third bar.

This chord is almost identical to a 'sus 2', as both feature a F# – the second or (counting beyond the octave) ninth note of an E minor scale. The difference between them is subtle but important: a 'sus 2' temporarily replaces its third (G in this case) with the suspended note (F#), while an 'add 9' chord includes both 9th (F#) and third.

Exercise three, in E major, demonstrates how dominant 7ths can generate a cycle of chords, taking the listener on the musical equivalent of a 'scenic route' from B (the dominant of E), via G#, C# minor, F# minor and B (again) to the tonic. You'll already know some of the fingerings used here; one new shape, 'F#m 7', in bar 5, is produced by

Below: G#, C# and E: the notes for the partial 'A maj7' in bar 1 of Exercise 2 (the root A is missing, but implied by the chord's context), played on the 4th, 3rd and 2nd strings.

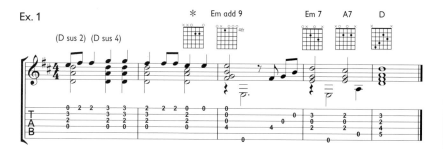

Ex. 1

Our second, A major piece is designed with the extra sustain of an electric guitar in mind. It lies almost entirely on the 2nd, 3rd and 4th strings, using a succession of 6th, major 7th and minor chords, and (in bars 3 and 4) a simple two-string motif which you play by sliding your second and third fingers up the fretboard, as indicated by the tablature.

Above: *The chord at the end of bar 2 here is a simple harmony with a complicated name: 'D maj 7 add 9'!

Ex. 2

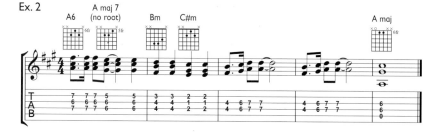

Right: Hold down the A6 and C#m shapes in this exercise with your second finger on the 4th string, your index on the 3rd string, and your third on the 2nd string. For the first A maj7 (shown in the photograph above) and Bm chords, use (in ascending order from 4th to 2nd strings) your second, third and index.

barréing across the top four strings at the 2nd fret to form the notes E, A, C# and F#.

Below: Remember that bracketed fingering dots on the chord diagrams indicate barrés, and that the 'fr' numbers alongside the grids correspond to fret numbers.

Ex. 3

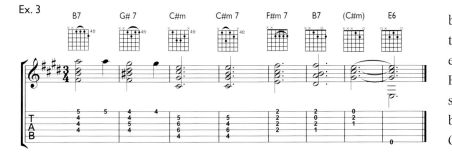

because, using the same logic the we applied to the naming of the 'Em add 9' harmony earlier, D is the '9th' note in the scale of C. For the chord in bar 4, you just slide the C7 shape down to the 1st fret, and the last three bars shouldn't cause many difficulties. Good luck!

Don't be alarmed by the ledger lines in the first three bars of Exercise 4 – or by the fact that, although the key signature reveals it to be in F major, it seems to start in G or C! The fingerings it requires are reasonably straightforward, and, in the first two bars, only the highest pairs of notes actually need to be fretted; the lower G and D are open strings. The basic chord shape required for bar 3 is an abbreviated C7 (see diagram and photo), to which, for the first two beats, you add a D from the first string with your third finger (making it, temporarily, C9 – so-called

Ex. 4

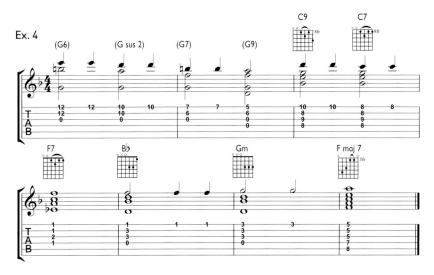

Above left: The start of Exercise 4, with the 2nd and 1st strings fretted at the 12th position to produce B and E, while the 3rd string is played open.

Left: The first chord of bar 2 in Exercise 4; note the position of the index finger, which is preparing to fret A at the 5th fret/1st string.

Above: The small-barréd 'C9' in bar 3 of Exercise 4; removing the third finger from the 10th fret/1st string will convert the chord to a simple C7.

Minor Key Exercises

Like the major-key exercises featured a little earlier, the four short musical examples below will give you the opportunity of trying out, in various keys and harmonic contexts, some of the chords we have just described.

The first of our pieces is in E minor, and uses only the lowest three fret positions; however, it poses quite a few technical challenges. In the opening bar, consisting of an A minor/A min6/A min7/A min6 progression, your little finger has to reach for the F# and G on the top string without disrupting the other digits, which are holding down the unchanging lower notes; while beneath the suspended chords in bars 2 and 3 are sustained basses that you must avoid damping with your fingers or your pick. The penultimate bar contains a C maj7 harmony, which resolves to E minor's relative major, G.

Left: The second chord in bar one of Exercise 1; after playing a standard A minor shape, the fourth finger holds down the F# (2nd fret/1st string) that turns the harmony into 'Am 6'.

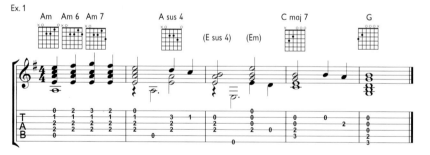

The chords in Exercise 2 are sparse, and occasionally (theoretically speaking) incomplete, lacking thirds and 'proper' basses. Nevertheless, guitar parts of this kind can make a powerful impact, particularly when played aggressively, with a bright, edgy tone. To get the right effect, select the back pickup if you're using an electric; on an acoustic, strike the strings a little closer to the bridge. The exercise is in G minor, and requires small barrés for its root and A major chords.

Right: The third chord in the same bar of Ex. 1. Here, the little finger has moved up to G (3rd fret/1st string), and the result is 'Am 7'.

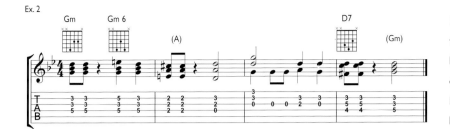

Ex. 2

Below: This is the opening 'D sus 2' shape in Ex. 3. The third finger plays D (7th fret/3rd string), and the index barrés across the 2nd and 1st strings to produce E and A. The bass D is supplied by the open 4th string. Move the fingers down two frets to play the notes in bar 2.

Exercise 3 is slower, and in the unfamiliar time signature of 2/2 (two minims per bar). The notes in the first bar 'add up' to a chord of 'D sus 2', produced by the left-hand shape shown in the diagram and photo, accompanied by a bass D from the open 4th string. At the start of bar 2, this shape is slid down two frets to create a 'G sus 4' harmony. The second and fourth quavers in bar 3 are 'pull-offs' similar to those you encountered in a previous exercise; instead of striking them with the pick, sound them by lifting your left-hand finger clear of the preceding notes a little more vigorously than normal.

Ex. 3

Our final exercise starts off easy, and gets progressively trickier! It's in B minor, and incorporates root, F# minor, E minor and D shapes before reaching a fuller sounding, four string added 9th chord in bar 5. A convenient alternative to trying to fret the bass F# in bar 8 with your index finger would be to hold this note down with your left-hand thumb – though this useful method of playing low notes may fill classical guitarists, and their teachers, with horror!

Above: The pull-offs in bar 3 (see main text) are played by the third finger, which frets and then releases the slurred A and E quavers on (respectively) the 1st and 2nd strings, while the index maintains its barré at the 3rd fret.

Ex. 4

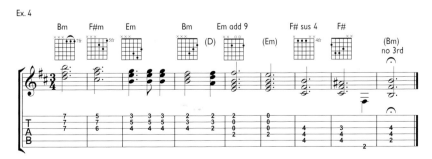

Above: The second, third and fourth fingers line up to play the chord in bar 7 of Ex. 4.

What You've Learned

* In this chapter, we've focused on the three most important scales in popular and classical music: the **major**, and the **melodic** and **harmonic minors**.

* Many of the fingering patterns you've learned for these can be used in a variety of neck positions to produce major and minor scales in different keys.

* The 'one-fret-per-finger' method, in which individual left-hand digits are 'assigned' to all the notes at a given fret position, is the basis for most scale- and melody-playing on the guitar – although it's sometimes necessary to 'cheat' by stretching across two or more frets to reach particular notes.

* The bass (root) notes of the harmonies comprising the 'three-chord trick' come from the first (**tonic**), fourth (**subdominant**), and fifth (**dominant**) degrees of the major or minor scale.

* The major scale's **relative minor** chord is formed from its sixth (**submediant**) degree.

* The minor scale's **relative major** chord is formed from its third (**mediant**) degree.

* By adding and substituting notes, you can create **suspended**, **major 7th** and **dominant 7th** chords from basic majors and minors.

Chapter 5
The 12-Bar Blues

The blues has been described as a metaphorical 'chair' supporting almost every pop and rock composer and songwriter; and its influence is inextricably linked to that of the guitar. W.C. Handy (1873-1958), the African-American composer and transcriber known as the 'Father of the Blues', was himself a guitarist; while the instrument's cheapness and portability made it a natural choice for the itinerant pre-World War II bluesmen, such as Robert Johnson (1911-1938) and Bukka White (1906-1977), who laid the foundations for much of the music's subsequent development. Later figures like Muddy Waters (1915-1983) and Bukka White's cousin B.B. King (b.1925) went on to inspire numerous rock players with their powerful, innovative use of the electric guitar; and, as a result, blues-derived harmonies, licks and riffs have become an inescapable part of today's musical mainstream. This chapter provides an elementary introduction to the genre's basic chords and scale patterns.

The '12-Bar' and the 'Shuffle'

This book is designed to teach you how to play, not what to play: but here we make an exception by exploring the basics of the blues – an idiom you're almost certain to encounter as a guitarist, either in its 'pure' acoustic and electric versions, or via jazz, rock and pop, all of which borrow extensively from its chord sequences and distinctive soloing styles.

The simplest, and most commonly used blues structure is the so-called '12-bar blues'. The '12-bar' begins with four bars of a tonic chord, followed by two bars of a subdominant, and a return to the tonic for two further bars. It then moves to the dominant for a single bar, down to the subdominant for another bar, and concludes with a bar each of tonic and dominant, before starting again. However, such a bald explanation doesn't begin to do justice to the almost infinite possibilities of this apparently rudimentary cycle of harmonies. The 12-bar is a musical chameleon, which can be transformed by the imaginative use of rhythm, melody and additional chords. It has provided the basis for thousands of songs – from Glenn Miller's 'In The Mood' to Chuck Berry's 'Johnny B. Goode' – and, though it's been around for the best part of a century, it remains a major inspiration for countless performers.

Let's prepare to play the blues by mastering the 'shuffle' – one of the genre's stock-in-trades – and learning how to embellish its chords with some 6ths and dominant 7ths. Here, first, is a shortened and slightly simplified 'two-string' version of the 'shuffle'. (The notation for it appears on the right.) While this dotted rhythm is fairly easy to manage, it's only a rough approximation of

a 'real' shuffle, which subdivides each crotchet beat into *three*, using what musicians call **triplets**; these are notated with a bracket marked '3' above the notes (see opposite). To play them, try counting '**1**-2-3 **2**-2-3 **3**-2-3 **4**-2-3' (the first number in each group should fall on the bar's successive crotchet beats), and placing the initial tripleted notes on these main beats, and the second note in each pair on '-3'.

The triplet subdivision makes the second note of each group slightly longer than a 'real' quaver beat would be, creating a distinctive, slightly weightier rhythmic feel that you're sure to recognize from blues and rock records. Try it out for yourself in the following exercise, which contains some denser chords than its predecessor (see the diagrams for their fingerings); you'll then be ready for a fully-fledged '12-bar' sequence.

Above: The C#s and D naturals in the first two bars of this exercise are played by the second and third fingers on the 2nd string; all Bs and Es are, of course, open. In bars 3 and 4, hold down the C#s (2nd fret/2nd string) with your second finger, and fret the F#s and Gs on the 1st string with (respectively) your third and fourth fingers.

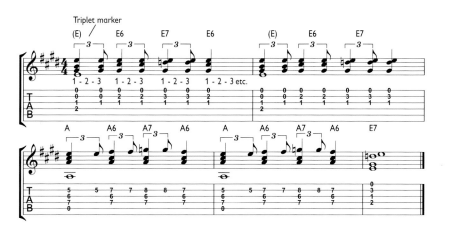

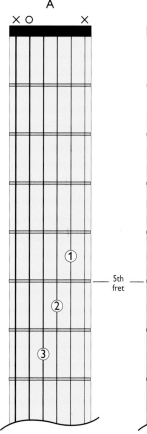

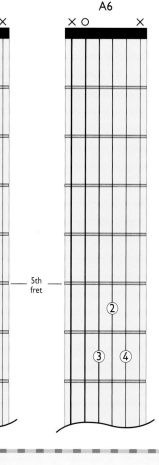

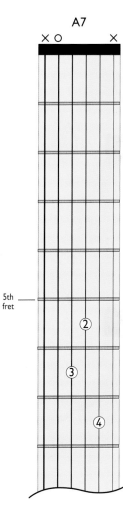

THREE GIANTS OF BLUES GUITAR

To appreciate the range and emotional power of the blues, check out the music of these three all-time greats:

B. B. King (b. 1925)

King made his early reputation in Memphis, and subsequently built up a huge following for his distinctive brand of blues – appearing all over the world with his own band, and also collaborating with leading rock performers such as Eric Clapton and Van Morrison. His intense, yet beautifully controlled vocals and solo guitar work can be heard at their peak on the album *Live at the Regal*, recorded in 1964.

John Lee Hooker (c.1919-2001)

Hooker's songs, often based around repeated chords and riffs rather than standard 12-bar structures, had an elemental, hypnotic quality, earning him the nickname 'The Boogie Man'. A cult figure for much of his earlier career, he achieved wider recognition in his seventies and eighties, thanks to Grammy-winning albums like *The Healer* (1989) and *Don't Look Back* (1997).

Stevie Ray Vaughan (1954-1990)

SRV's potent, strongly rock-influenced style brought him massive audiences and a string of awards and gold discs. After bursting onto the scene with *Texas Flood* (1983), the band he led, Double Trouble, recorded and toured tirelessly throughout the rest of the decade. Their career was cut short by Stevie Ray's tragic death in a helicopter crash in August 1990.

Your First 12-Bar

Passages like the one in the last exercise can certainly drive along a blues rhythm, but may sound too 'busy' in some contexts. The 12-bar you're going to try now has a more 'laid-back' feel, though it still retains an insistent 'shuffle' beat. You'll probably want to begin by playing it quite slowly; however, it also works well at faster speeds, and is equally appropriate for acoustic or electric guitar.

At first glance, the notation for this blues, with its triplets and tied notes, may seem intimidating; but in fact, the piece itself is quite straightforward. As it's in A major, it can make extensive use of the instrument's three open bass strings, and most of the notes above them are produced using simple variants of familiar, nut-position shapes. The chords for the first two bars switch between A7 and E minor fingerings (see notation and photos), followed, in bars 3 and 4, by a small-barréd A7 that converts to 'A6' (A major with an F# on top) when you release your second finger from the G at the 3rd fret on the 1st string.

These harmonies bring us to the 'subdominant' part of the 12-bar. The basic chord here is D7, with the top string once again supplying a little variety by taking us to 'D7 sus 2' and 'D7 sus 4' – both of which swiftly resolve back to D7. In bar 7, we return to the tonic, with the 'home' A7 shape spiced up by a momentary shift to 'Am 7', created by the C natural played on the 1st fret/2nd string.

Ringing the changes

After bars 9 and 10, featuring (respectively) E7/E6 and D7/D7 sus 2 shapes, we approach the last few bars of the blues – the section known as the 'turnaround', leading either to another 12-bar cycle, or (as here) to the conclusion. It's customary, at this point, to

introduce some alternative chords into the regular tonic/dominant sequence; and accordingly, bar 11 includes a D major/D minor harmony as it leads us to the number's coda.

Above: The transition from E minor (with an open A bass) back to A7 in bars 1 and 2 is triggered by the third finger, which converts the open 2nd (B) string to a C# at the 2nd fret.

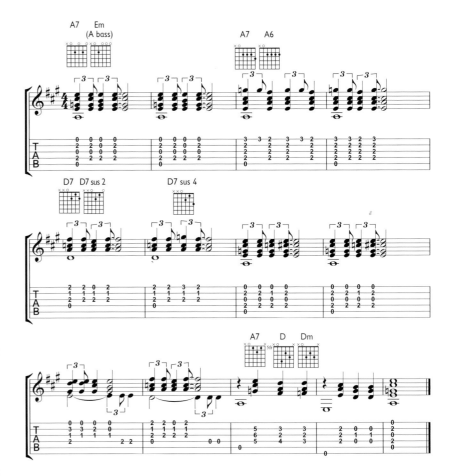

Above: Less familiar shapes in this exercise have diagrams above them; see photographs above and opposite for the fingerings needed to play the marked chords in bars 1, 3, and 11.

100

Right: Another 'one-finger' chord change: this 2nd fret barré, plus a G held down by the second finger at the 3rd fret, equals A7…

Right: …but without the G, the result is A6.

Above: The D minor chord on the last beat in bar 11 of exercise 1: the 6th and 1st strings are not sounded here.

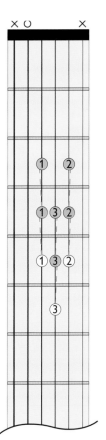

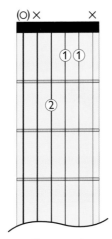

Experienced blues performers will generally insert something more elaborate and adventurous at the turnaround – like the progressions in the alternative conclusion to our blues shown below. Its quaver triplets and final chord both contain new harmonies, which we'll be examining in detail overleaf.

Below: This 'substitute' ending can be used to replace bars 9-12 above. The adjacent diagrams will help you with its 'turnaround' sequence.

Diagram 1

Diagram 2

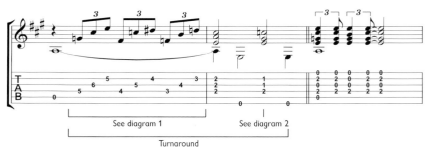

Above: Follow these descending patterns of first, second and third finger placings (starting at the 5th and 6th frets, and then sliding down to the 4th/5th, and the 3rd/4th frets, as shown) to play the triplet quavers in bar 3 of the second example.

Above: When fingering this unfamiliar chord, featured in bar 3 of Example 2, it doesn't matter if your index touches the 1st string when making its small barré on the 1st fret/2nd and 3rd strings – so long as you don't actually sound it!

101

Chapter 6
More Advanced Techniques

Over the previous chapters, you've discovered quite a lot about the standard left- and right-hand techniques adopted by the majority of steel-strung guitar players. Now, though, it's time for a glimpse at a few widely used alternatives to these methods. First, we try out some 'fingerstyle' exercises, in which the strings are struck directly with the thumb, index, middle and ring fingers of the right hand (the little finger is omitted, due to its small size and comparative weakness). We go on to experiment with altering the pitches of the instrument's open tunings – an approach that generates rich sonorities and sustain, though it also makes most 'regular' chord shapes useless! And we end by learning how to produce the ringing, high-pitched tones known as harmonics... a more conventional, but highly dramatic trick of the guitarist's trade.

Fingerpicking Basics

For the next few pages, we're going to put aside the flat-pick and focus on fingerstyle playing – a method of sounding the strings that's especially favoured by acoustic guitarists, though it also has its devotees among electric axemen.

Below – Photograph 1: Suggested right-hand nail lengths for fingerstyle playing.

Bottom – Photograph 2: This shows the basic right-hand fingerstyle position.

Its biggest advantage is the freedom it gives to strike non-adjacent strings simultaneously; thanks to this, fingerstylists can create elaborate combinations of melodies, harmonies and basslines, and deploy a number of more specialized techniques, like the multi-digit *rasgueado* effects used in flamenco. Many performers also find it easier to generate and control subtle gradations of tone with their bare fingers – even though an evening's vigorous picking without a plectrum can exact a high price in broken nails!

To minimize such damage, and produce as clean and powerful a fingerstyle sound as possible, you should trim (or grow!) the nails on your right-hand fingers and thumb so that they extend about a couple of millimetres beyond the ends of their respective digits (see photograph 1). When preparing to play, position them parallel to the strings as shown in photograph 2, with your third finger close to the 1st string, and your second and index over the 2nd and 3rd strings; we won't be using the little finger. Your thumb should be able to reach any of the three bottom strings; try sounding the open 6th (E) string with it in a downstroke-type movement (keeping your wrist still), and then move your index upwards (away from the floor) to pick the 3rd (G). Though the tips of your finger and thumb will touch the strings momentarily, your nails should bear the brunt of the contact with them; this combination produces a mixture of hard attack and warmer, softer timbre.

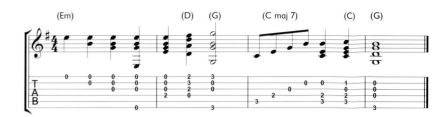

crotchet chords by br
strings with a downst
finger. Once again, let
ring on as much as y

Making strategic use
strings when fingerpic
create parts that are l
and fast-moving. The
derives its 'singing' qu
bass notes, but from t

Once these two notes are sounding cleanly, have a go at the exercise on the right, which involves all six strings. While getting accustomed to fingerstyle, it may help to think of your right hand as a claw, with fingers and thumb converging on the strings as they strike them. Remember that the 1st, 2nd and 3rd string notes are played using the upward finger movement described in the last paragraph, while the thumb travels in the opposite direction. Make sure that all the notes are sounded evenly and on the beat, and allow the opening quavers of the 'C maj 7' harmony (see notation) ring on by keeping the C and E (5th and 4th strings) held down throughout the bar. Don't strum any of the chords!

Above – Photograph 3: In this photograph, the right hand has just struck the E minor chord at the end of the first bar of the exercise.

Left – Photograph 4: Picking the 'C maj 7' harmony in bar 3.

struck repeatedly in its
should be left to resona
Bar 5 contains a succe
intervals (C/A, B/G, A/
and 3rd strings. These
manage, and create a p
favoured by both folk p
guitar composers!

The last few pieces hav
of the simpler possibilit
and some guitarists (no
songwriters' mentioned
beyond the rudimentar
string basslines we've b
However, fingerpicking
extensive and adventure
can get a brief taste of
following pages.

THE ROOTS OF FINGERSTYLE

Fingerstyle was originally developed by 17th- and 18th-century classical guitarists, who played gut-strung instruments with their fingertips. Later musicians found that fingernails produced a clearer, more powerful tone, and the 'nails-only' method eventually became the norm in classical circles, largely due to its adoption by Andrés Segovia (1893-1987). (Segovia was also an early advocate and endorsee of strings made from nylon, a better-sounding, longer lasting alternative to gut; these are now fitted to almost all 'Spanish'-style guitars.)

By the late 1930s, a handful of steel-strung players – mostly American folk, country and blues performers inspired by banjo-pickers – were creating their own distinctive versions of fingerstyle. The numbers of these guitarists (and the variety of their right-hand techniques!) have grown steadily since then. Some favour fingertips, others 'tips-and-nails', while those seeking maximum volume often attach metal or plastic finger- and thumb picks to their striking hands – another approach borrowed from the banjo.

Ele
Exe

Fingerpicki
especially
full-sounding
simple way o
chord-based l
something the
a plectrum, a:
reached with

Our first exercise
introduction or c
acoustic-style son
and contains recu
which 'add up' to
suspended harmo
The moving crote
and B, followed b
G) are all produce
left-hand shape. F
three different ne
bars 1-2, 3-4 and
broken chords.

What You've Learned

* Fingerstyle playing allows you to pick almost any combination of strings simultaneously; these don't have to be adjacent to each other, as they do when using a plectrum.

* It's especially suitable for accompanying singers, and for elaborate solo pieces featuring melodies, chords and basslines.

* As a general rule, use your right-hand thumb to strike the three lowest strings, and your first, second and third fingers for (respectively) the 3rd, 2nd and 1st strings. In some guitar music, right-hand fingerings are indicated by single-letter abbreviations next to the notes and chords: **p** (pulgar) for thumb, **i** for index, **m** for middle (second), and **a** (annular) for third.

* Notes from open strings, especially in the bass, can 'smooth over' chord changes, and provide support for melodies and licks. Open tunings (like 'dropped G' or 'open E') maximize this sustaining effect, though they aren't so useful for chords that don't include the pitches supplied by their unfretted strings.

* Harmonics can 'spice up' solos, riffs and chords; artificial harmonics can be created by fretting a string, and then touching it twelve, seven or five frets above the position where it's being held down.

Chapter 7
Where To Now?

Now that you've almost reached the end of this book, it's time to take stock of what you've learned, to decide on your musical and technical goals – and to consider the current state and future suitability of the gear you're using. This chapter suggests various ways in which you can improve your instrument's sound and playability, and outlines the options open to you if you choose to upgrade it, or add outboard equipment like effects pedals and recording devices. It also tells you where to find advanced tutor books, videos, and other study guides that will boost your development as a player, and provides a little practical advice on the pleasures and pitfalls of rehearsing and performing with fellow musicians.

Choosing and Changing Strings

After spending so many hours with your guitar, you'll now be thoroughly familiar with the shape of its neck and body, and the way it responds to your touch. You may also have begun to notice a few shortcomings and imperfections in its performance; and the first part of this chapter looks at some of the ways in which these can be remedied. A good way to start the process is to give your instrument a fresh set of strings – an inexpensive improvement that's guaranteed to bring a new sparkle to its sound.

During their short life (which varies from a few days to several months, depending on frequency of use and other factors), strings absorb sweat and grease from your left hand, become coated in dust, and endure lengthy periods of pounding from your plectrum while stretched to high tensions. All this leads to a gradual deterioration in their tone quality and physical condition; and eventually, badly worn strings may corrode, unwind, or simply break.

Hopefully, your strings haven't yet reached these dire straits, but by now, they're almost certainly overdue for renewal. If you didn't buy a spare set with your guitar, read the panel opposite to help you choose the correct type and gauge, then head down to your local music shop to obtain them. The other essential tools for restringing are your pitch pipes, electronic tuner or other pitch reference, and a small pair of wire cutters.

Don't remove all six old strings at once, as this may damage your guitar. Instead, begin by slackening off the 'used' 1st string until it can easily be unthreaded from the **capstan** on the machine head. *Its end is very sharp: be*

Above: Detaching a used 5th string from the bridge of a Fender Telecaster.

especially careful to keep it away from your eyes. To detach the string completely from an electric, push it out through the hole anchoring its ball-end to the guitar's body or tailpiece. On acoustics, the ball-end is usually held in place by a bridge-pin, which you must pull out to release the string.

STRING TYPES AND GAUGES

Most strings designed for electric guitars are made from high-grade steel, overlaid, on the 4th, 5th and 6th strings, with nickel windings. For acoustics, steel with bronze windings is generally preferred, and acoustic string sets usually include a wound 3rd, giving an extra boost to their tone.

Your guitar (whether electric or acoustic) was almost certainly fitted with **light gauge** strings by its manufacturer. String gauges are defined by their diameters, measured in decimal fractions of an inch. A typical 'light gauge' acoustic set contains a 1st string with a diameter of .011", and a 6th of about .052" (with other strings in proportion). Electric strings are normally slightly thinner, featuring a light gauge 1st of approximately .010", and a 6th of .046"; **extra light** sets, with 1st string diameters of as little as .008", are also widely used.

Lighter strings are easy on the fingers, and require less effort to bend; however, for a richer, more powerful sound and a more solid overall 'feel', try experimenting with **medium gauge** acoustic or electric sets: these will often have 1st strings of about .013", and 6ths of .056". A variety of custom gauges and special windings and coatings is also available.

Above: Fitting a new string – 1: the string is fed into a hole at the back of the Telecaster that leads up to the instrument's bridge assembly. The ball-end is held in place inside the Tele's body; other guitars have tailpieces or combined bridge/tailpiece blocks to retain the strings.

Replacing the strings

Attach your new 1st string to an electric by threading it through the body or tailpiece until the ball-end stops it from moving any further; on acoustics, push the ball-end into the bridge, and press the bridge-pin firmly down on top of it. Now, thread and wind the string's other end onto the capstan as shown in the photograph, turning the machine head to take up the slack and raise the pitch. Watch out for slippage and snagging, and on acoustics, make sure that the bridge-pin stays in place as you increase the tension. Use the other strings and/or your external pitch reference to check the tuning of the new string, which will remain unstable for several minutes until it's fully unstretched. Finally, use your wire cutters to trim its protruding end from the machine head...before repeating the entire procedure for the other five strings!

Left: Fitting a new string – 2: the string is threaded through the capstan, and tightened by turning the machine head. At the start of this process, the loose string is difficult to keep in position; holding it down with a finger (as illustrated) will make it easier to wind.

Set-ups, Modifications and Upgrades

Even after you've changed strings and gauges, you may find that your guitar still isn't working as well as you'd like. Does its action remain uncomfortable? Have the frets become worn or damaged? Do the notes and chords you play in higher positions seem slightly out of tune relative to those lower down the neck? In the weeks or months since you bought it, has it developed any new buzzes, rattles, or (if it's an electric) clicks and hums from its pickups, control knobs, or switches?

Below: Expensive guitars like this one boast better overall build quality and more powerful, richer-sounding pickups than their budget-priced counterparts.

Time for a new guitar?

If the answer to one or more of these questions is 'yes', it may be worth taking your acoustic or electric in for a 'set-up'. (Most guitar shops offer this service, or can recommend an experienced local technician who provides it.) 'Setting-up' involves adjusting the instrument's string and fret height to match your preferences and choice of string gauges, optimizing its intonation, and diagnosing and remedying other minor and not-so-minor snags. 'Techs' will also be happy to discuss more radical upgrades and modifications: it's usually easy for them to replace the pickups on cheaper electric guitars with better, higher-output components, or to fit a new bridge or tremolo system which may transform a mediocre instrument into something special. And if you'd like to be able to play your acoustic through an amplifier, or into a tape machine or effects unit, without using a microphone, ask about having a **piezo-electric pickup** installed in it: these are available at quite reasonable prices, and won't affect the 'unplugged' sound of the instrument.

However, there are limits to what even the most skilled tech can accomplish. While any axe can benefit from a few performance-enhancing tweaks, bolted-on extras can never make a silk purse out of a 'sow's ear' electric; and there's even less scope for improving cheap acoustics, whose laminated bodies simply can't match the superior sound provided by models built from higher-quality tonewoods. A reputable tech will give you a fair and honest assessment of what can and can't be done to get more out of your guitar; and his verdict may lead you to consider selling it, and buying (or saving up for!) something better. When doing so, always try to dispose of your old instrument privately, rather than accepting a part-exchange deal; this will almost invariably leave you with more cash in hand to seek out the guitar of your dreams!

Above: A little unscrewing and soldering are all that would be required to upgrade the pickups and controls on this Korean-made electric.

Left: A top-of-the-range solid-body with several interesting extras – including a special pickup (mounted below its bridge) allowing it to interface with a synthesizer.

Learning More

With the knowledge of scales, chords, right-hand techniques and elementary theory you've already acquired, and your guitar set up to your satisfaction (or a more suitable instrument in your arms!), you're ready to embark on a new, fascinating stage in your musical journey – one whose direction you'll determine by deciding which kind of music you're most interested in, and how you want to apply your guitar-playing skills to it.

Below: 'Miking up' is one simple way to compensate for the differing levels of acoustic and electric guitars, though it may lead to problems with feedback – the howling sound generated when amplified sound finds its way back into the microphone.

While getting to grips with your chosen style, you'll be able to make use of a huge range of printed music, CDs and technological assistance. A few decades ago, budding jazz guitarists would have struggled to decipher fast-moving solos by 'greats' such as Django Reinhardt or Tal Farlow. (One tortuous method of achieving this was to slow down vinyl LPs of their playing from 33 to 16 rpm – causing a dramatic pitch drop as well as a reduction in tempo – in an attempt to catch every semiquaver.) Today, you can buy or borrow notation and tablature transcriptions of all their classic numbers, and of similarly influential compositions by other top blues and jazz artists, from Robert Johnson to Pat Metheny ...though actually managing to play them remains as great a challenge as ever!

Lovers of rock guitar may not find it so easy to find printed versions of their idols' riffs and licks (though there's a growing range of books, magazine articles and videos that explain 'how they're done'); but here, digital technology can come to the rescue, in the shape of 'phrase trainers' like the Tascam model shown opposite. These allow you to insert a CD featuring a favourite solo, sample and 'loop' it, slow it down without dropping its pitch, plug in your guitar, and play along with the repeated, reduced-speed phrase(s) until you can copy them note-for-note.

HOW DO YOU...

Learn the classic songs used in jazz, and discover more about the work of the great jazz guitarists?

So-called 'fake books' – anthologies of jazz 'standards', showing melody lines, lyrics, and chords, are widely available.

Look for CD compilations of jazz players you're interested in, and check out specialist retailers and mail-order outlets for books containing transcriptions of their solos.

Begin to study blues playing styles?

Listen to your favourite artists.

Read histories of the music, and find recordings of the guitarists whose stories they tell.

Learn from printed tutors/transcription books/videos – those by top American guitarist Stefan Grossman are especially useful when studying slide techniques and alternative tunings (Grossman acquired his own skills directly from blues and gospel greats like Rev. Gary Davis).

Emulate your favourite rock guitarist?

Consider using a phrase trainer (see opposite).

Buy or borrow songbooks and sheet music.

Read leading UK and (especially) US guitar magazines containing regular features on top performers, their gear and their playing techniques.

Learn more about electronic effects.

Another useful tool for practice, study, and sharing your musical ideas with others is some kind of audio recording device. Once, most of us relied on 'lo-fi' cassette machines, which could only capture sound in 'real time'; then came the TEAC 'Portastudio'™ and its many imitators (allowing simple multitracking and mixing), followed, eventually, by the emergence of the first reasonably-priced digital recorders. These now range from Minidiscs, which can be combined with a stereo microphone to record your rehearsals, to multitrackers that can help you create elaborate, richly layered soundscapes from a single guitar.

Machines like these, boasting a plethora of powerful electronic effects, can provide an enticing virtual environment for the lone musician; and some users, having once connected their instruments and headphones to them, tend to become 'bedroom' players, rarely involving themselves in live performance. However, more gregarious guitarists with a taste for gigging shouldn't dismiss technology as something that's just for home- or studio-based experiments. As we shall see, pedals and other sound processors have been shaping the guitar's onstage sound for decades, and are currently more popular, versatile and inexpensive than ever before.

Above: TASCAM's CD-GT1 phrase trainer enables you to sample and practise difficult riffs and solos taken from recordings. It also includes high-quality digital effects.

Left: The 4-track TASCAM Pocketstudio 5 records digitally to Compact Flash media; completed songs can be transferred to a computer via its USB port.

135

Effects-2

Guitar effects come in a variety of shapes and sizes – some as pedals, others as rack-mountable, studio-style boxes – but they must all be interconnected, provided with mains or battery power, and, of course, plugged into your guitar (at one end) and your amp (at the other).

Even a small number of them can create a tangle of wires, and an array of knobs and switches that require distracting amounts of tweaking and toggling; and the sight and sound of the 'over-effected' onstage musician has often attracted ridicule from audiences and critics ...most famously in the *New Musical Express*, whose 'Lone Groover' cartoon strip once portrayed an especially foolish-looking guitarist posing in front of the pile of equipment he allegedly needed to be 'ready to play the blues'.

Though excessive users of electric guitar effects may sometimes be figures of fun, their array of gear does, at least, give them direct control over their own 'live' sound. Until relatively recently, acoustic pickers weren't in this happy position: before the advent of low-distortion amp/speaker combos, specially

Above: Ovation has been a leading maker of pickup-equipped acoustic guitars since the 1970s. Like all its instruments, the 1779 Custom Legend seen here has a bowlbacked body made from a synthetic material, Lyrachord; its spruce top is decorated with abalone. See opposite below for a photo of its shoulder-mounted preamplifier.

Left: The Laney LA65C combo is specially designed for acoustic instruments. It has built-in chorus and reverb, and provides a 65-watt output through two 8in (20.3cm) speakers; it also boasts a horn driver to handle high frequency audio signals.

Left: Marshall's AS100D combo, created, as the company's publicity puts it, 'for the acoustic player who wants it all.' Each of its stereo channels is rated at 50 watts, and it incorporates extensive onboard effects, as well as equalization and anti-feedback controls.

designed to handle the output from their microphones or piezo-electric pickups, their instrument signals were sent straight to the PA (Public Address) system in the venues where they played. Here, volume, equalization, compression and reverb were in the hands of a house engineer (or, all too frequently, some poorly trained 'jobsworth') with little knowledge or appreciation of the guitarist's requirements, and the results could be dire. Nowadays, acoustic-oriented amps like those mentioned above are much more common, and the instruments themselves usually contain sophisticated **preamplifiers** and equalizers, permitting the sound from their onboard **transducers** to be boosted and shaped at source.

The latest generation of amplifiers and processors for both acoustic and electric guitars make growing use of digital wizardry. Low-quality analogue devices (such as the traditional 'spring reverb': a box with a wire spring inside, which produced a twanging echo, often accompanied by a range of unwanted additional noises) are being replaced by microchips, whose power and versatility allow the creation and combination of multiple effects in a single box – finally solving the Lone Groover's 'interconnection' problem! Even relatively cheap units of this kind can offer hundreds of different sounds; many also feature 'digital modelling technology', which stores the simulated tonal characteristics of various 'classic' amps/speakers and guitar pickups, and can apply them to any incoming signal.

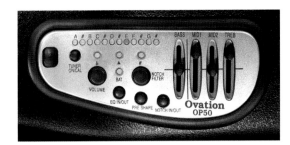

Left: The high performance OP50 preamplifier fitted to the Ovation 1779 Custom Legend, with 4-band equalization and a built-in electronic tuner.

Practising With Other Musicians

Though your own onstage debut may still be some time away, it isn't too soon to start thinking about how you and your guitar might interact with other musicians – maybe by swapping ideas or licks with one or two fellow-pickers, or by taking part in larger-scale collaborations alongside a range of different instruments. No matter how informal these sessions are going to be, it helps to plan them as thoroughly as possible.

Below: Joint rehearsal sessions can be an enjoyable way to develop your guitar-playing skills.

Opposite: It's only rock and roll… but we like it!

Make a list of the songs or items you want to tackle, provide copies of their chords for each participant, master any tricky solo passages and riffs beforehand…and consider the practicalities as well as the musical content. Is your chosen practice-room big enough? Does it have sufficient power points for amps and other gear? And, if you're combining acoustic and electric instruments, or including vocals, will everybody be audible? Generally speaking, singers and acoustic guitars need to be amplified when they're used alongside electric instruments and/or drums. (Spare guitar amps connected to suitable microphones, or even, at a pinch, a karaoke machine, can be pressed into service for this.) Don't attempt to use a home stereo, which won't be able to handle the high signal levels. However, an acoustic piano can usually hold its own against an electric guitar and even a percussionist, so long as the overall volume is kept fairly low.

You may well want to stand up during the rehearsal, even though it's harder to manage barrés and other complicated chords while doing so. To minimize discomfort, and keep your instrument properly supported, buy a strong, wide strap for your guitar, securing it firmly to the metal 'buttons' on the instrument's body. (Some acoustics have only one button; their straps should be tied to their headstocks, just above the nut.) Position the 'strapped-up' guitar at roughly the same height and angle you use when sitting, and don't be tempted to lower it to thigh or crotch level!

It may seem a little tedious to mention 'health and safety' aspects in this context, but any gathering of musicians with amplifiers can create electrical hazards, and generate dangerously high sound levels. Always ensure that the mains-powered equipment you use is in good order, and correctly earthed; if you have any doubts about the wiring in the place where you're playing, check the sockets you're using with a Martindale tester (see photograph); and keep drinks and other fluids well away from amps, microphones and plugged-in guitars. Don't practise for long periods at high volumes; stop immediately if you start to experience 'threshold shift' (a temporary reduction in the apparent sensitivity of your hearing, often accompanied by ringing in your ears); and remember that there's no generally accepted cure for tinnitus and other forms of aural impairment.

None of these dreary warnings should prevent you from having fun with other musicians – or do anything to reduce the adrenaline rush you'll experience when everyone's playing starts to gel, or when you turn up the volume to take your first solo. The excitement of such moments never wears off, and its enduring impact was summed up perfectly by the late Frank Zappa: 'I love to play the guitar. It's one of the great physical sensations of all time.'

Above: Use a Martindale tester to ensure that mains sockets are safe.

What You've Learned

* Change your guitar's strings before they become badly discoloured or corroded. As they age, they'll gradually lose their treble response; to avoid too noticeable a tonal difference when you replace them, it's a good idea to break new strings in for a few hours before using them seriously. Experiment with slightly heavier sets if you want to 'beef up' your sound.

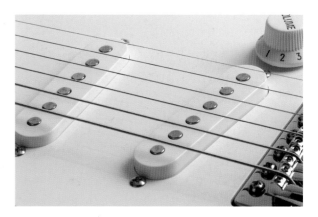

* Consult a dealer or technician about getting your instrument 'set up' to your personal requirements, and to find out if it would benefit from any modifications and additions. Target areas include **pickups** (these can be upgraded on electrics, or fitted as 'extras' to acoustics), the **bridge** and **nut** area (adjustments and refits here can improve the guitar's action and tone – and if you long for a 'whammy bar' on your electric, it's usually not too difficult to install a new bridge/tailpiece incorporating one), and the **neck** and **frets**. However, don't expect miracles from such 'tweaks'.

* Electronic effects will transform your sound (though not your playing style or musical ability), but powering them up and connecting them together can be time-consuming and fiddly, and it's easy to over-use them. If you decide to add one or more 'magic boxes' or pedals to your set-up, remember to switch them to 'bypass' sometimes!

* Stay up-to-date with current developments in the guitar world by reading one or more of the excellent monthly magazines devoted to the instrument. Leading American guitar magazines (most of which are easily available in Britain) can be a particularly valuable source of information about top musicians and new products; they carry extensive reviews and ads for guitar-related books, sheet music and videos.

Chord Dictionary

A major

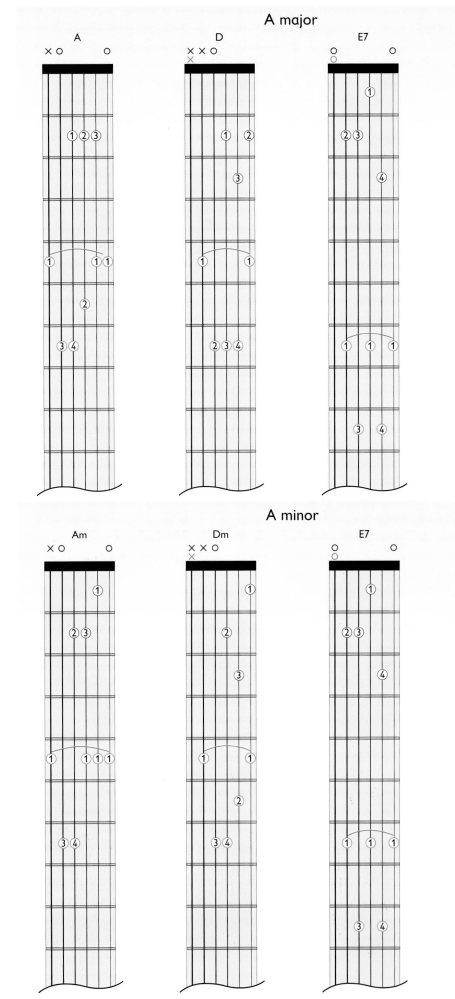

A minor

This dictionary gives the four most basic chords (tonic, subdominant, dominant 7th and relative minor/major) in all keys. Two shapes are shown for each chord: obviously, numerous alternative shapes may also be used. The keys of D♭ minor and A♭ minor are displayed in their enharmonic equivalents, C# minor and G# minor.

Bb major

Bb

Eb

F7

Gm

Bb minor

Bbm

Ebm

F7

Db

Chord Dictionary

Chord Dictionary

B major

B · E · F#7 · G#m

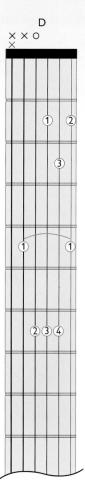

B minor

Bm · Em · F#7 · D

C major

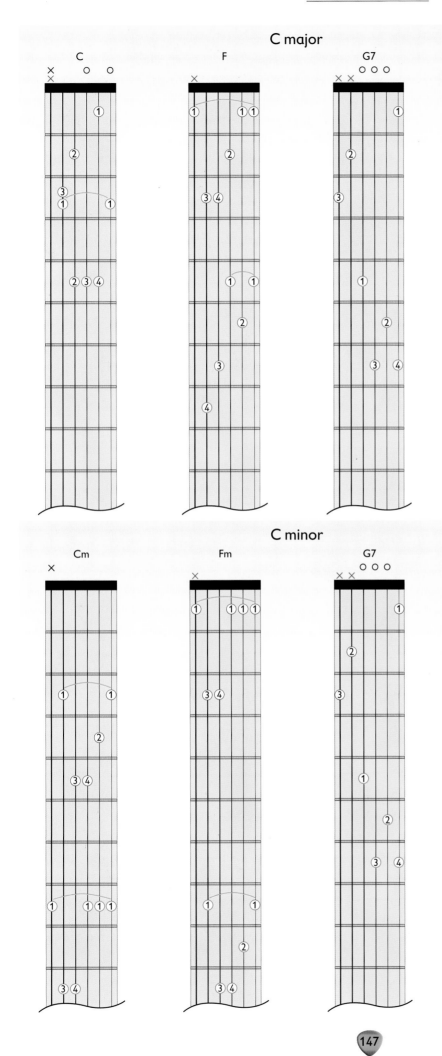

C minor

Chord Dictionary

Chord Dictionary

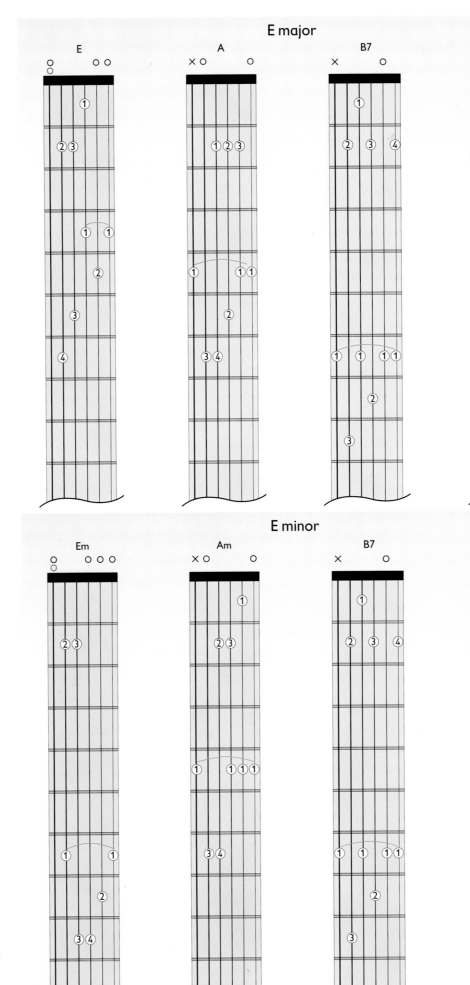

E major

E   A   B7   C#m *

E minor

Em   Am   B7   A7

* On lower chord, damp
4th string with the side
of your fourth finger.

E♭ major

E♭   A♭   B♭7   Cm

E♭ minor

E♭m   A♭m   B♭7   G♭

Chord Dictionary

Chord Dictionary

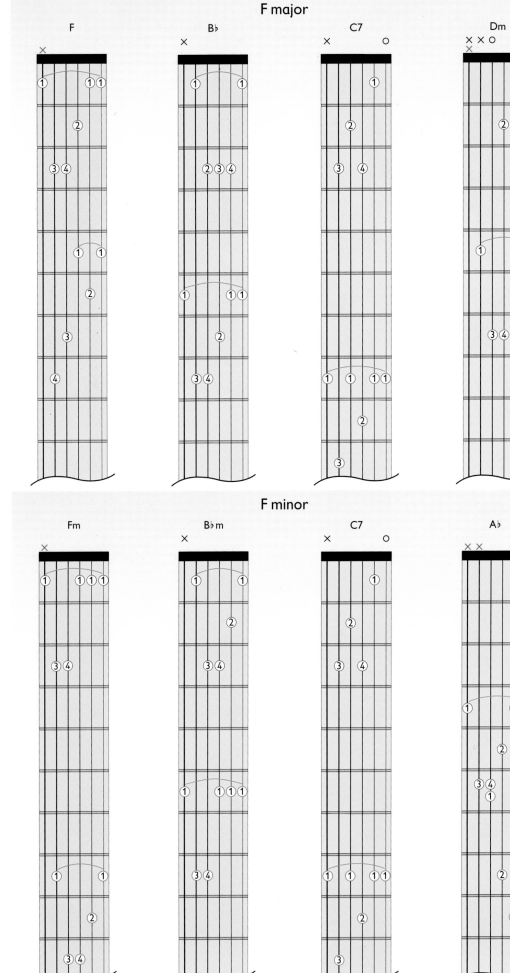

F major

| F | Bb | C7 | Dm |

F minor

| Fm | Bbm | C7 | Ab |

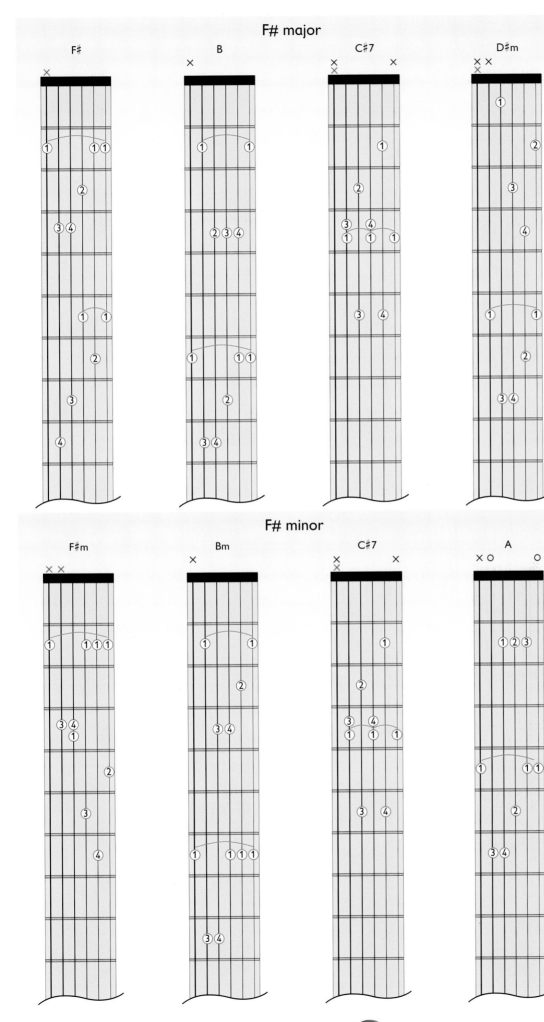

F# major

F#   B   C#7   D#m

F# minor

F#m   Bm   C#7   A

Chord Dictionary

Chord Dictionary

G major

G

C

D7

Em

G minor

Gm

Cm

D7

B♭

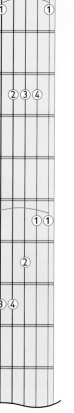

Ab major

Ab   Db   Eb7   Fm

G# minor

G#m   C#m *   D#7   B

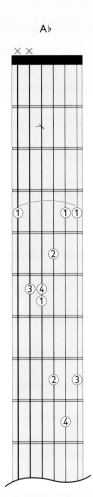

* On lower chord, damp
4th string with the side
of your fourth finger.

Chord Dictionary

155

Key signature
Group of sharp or flat symbols displayed immediately to the right of the clef in musical notation, indicating notes that must be consistently raised or lowered when playing in a specific key, and thus identifying the key itself.

Leading note
Seventh 'step' of a major or minor scale, separated by a semitone from the tonic note a degree above it.

Ledger lines
Horizontal lines used to indicate the pitch of notes that lie above or below the stave.

Lick
Memorable musical flourish from a guitar or other instrument, sometimes used as punctuation or as a springboard for a solo.

Machine heads
The mechanical, geared winding and tuning apparatus attached to the guitar's headstock.

Major
Type of chord, scale and key with an interval of four semitones (a major 3rd) between its root and third.

Minor
Chords, scales and keys with an interval of three semitones (a minor 3rd) between their roots and thirds.

Natural
Symbol (♮) used to cancel a preceding sharp or flat (in a key signature or nearby accidental) for the duration of a single bar.

Nut
Grooved block glued onto the neck between the headstock and the fingerboard, which sets the height and spacing of the strings as they pass down the instrument's body towards its bridge.

Octave
12-semitone interval, corresponding to an exact doubling in frequency, separating two or more notes of the same name.

Open string
String struck without being fretted. The standard 'open' pitches of the guitar's six strings are (from bottom to top) EADGBE.

Open tuning
Alternative pitches for the guitar's open strings, often forming a specific chord – i.e. 'open E' (EBEG#BE) or 'open G' (DGDGBD). (Tunings are shown from bottom to top.)

Pickup
Device that converts vibrations from a guitar's strings or body to electrical currents; these can then be fed through external amplification and/or recording equipment.

Pitch pipe
Simple reed-type device that can provide a handy pitch reference when tuning guitars and other instruments.

Plectrum, pick, flatpick
Sliver of plastic or other material, used to strike the steel strings of acoustic and electric guitars.

Relative major
Major key whose root is the third (mediant) note of a given minor scale. Relative majors share notes, chords, and key signatures with their associated minors.

Relative minor
Minor key whose root is the sixth (submediant) note of a given major scale. Relative minors share notes, chords, and key signatures with their associated majors.

Riff
Constantly repeated musical phrase (or close variant of it) underpinning a song or solo.

Semitone
The smallest officially recognized interval in Western music, corresponding to the change in pitch produced by moving between two adjacent frets on a guitar. Two semitones = one tone; twelve semitones = one octave.

Sharp
Term or symbol (#) applied to a note, indicating that it should be raised by a semitone. Also describes faulty tuning, resulting in notes or chords that are slightly too high in pitch.

Shuffle
Subdivision of a regular crotchet beat into triplets (giving four groups of three notes in a bar) used extensively in the blues.

Slide
Glass or metal cylinder worn on a guitarist's left-hand finger, and used (often in conjunction with open tunings) to produce pitch bends and glissandos on notes and chords.

Stack
Separate, vertically mounted amplifier box(es) and speaker cabinet(s) (cf. combo).

Stave
One or more groups of five horizontal lines onto which standard musical notation is written.

Strumming
Rapid, rhythmical down- or upstroke(s) across adjacent guitar strings.

Subdominant
The fourth 'step' in a major or minor scale, and the chord for which this note forms the root.

Suspension
Note from an adjacent or preceding chord, combined with another chord to create a pleasing musical 'clash'. See examples and exercises for suspended 2nds and 4ths (sus2, sus4).

Tablature, tab
Six-line representation of the guitar's strings/fingerboard, used as an alternative or supplement to standard musical notation.

Tailpiece
Most flat-tops and many electrics are fitted with bridges that also serve as an anchor for their strings. Other guitars, however, use a 'floating' bridge assembly, combined with a separate tailpiece (typically a metal or wooden trapeze-shaped unit or a steel block) to which the strings' ball-ends are fastened.

Three-chord trick
Nickname for the tonic, subdominant and dominant chords of a major or minor key –

the most commonly used harmonies in pop (and much other) music.

Tie
Curved line used in musical notation to indicate that two or more notes should be combined without a break between them.

Time signature
Two-figure code displayed at the start of a piece of musical notation, indicating the number and type of beats in each bar.

Tonic
The 'home-' or 'keynote' in a major or minor scale, and the chord for which it forms the root.

Top
The guitar's 'front' or 'face', onto which its strings and bridge are mounted.

Transducer
Pickup or similar device that turns one form of energy, such as the vibrations from a guitar string, into another – e.g. electrical current.

Tremolo
Strictly speaking, this Italian musical term refers to rapid fluctuations in the volume of a note or chord; but among guitarists, it is often used as a misnomer for vibrato (the term for pitch fluctuation), and many players call their instrument's vibrato units (a.k.a. whammy bars) 'tremolos' or 'trems.'

Turnaround
The last two bars of the 12-bar blues cycle, during which many players substitute more adventurous harmonies for the prescribed tonic and dominant chords.

Upstroke
Upward movement (i.e. away from floor) of plectrum/right hand when striking a note or chord on the guitar.

Vibrato unit, whammy bar
Mechanical unit, usually built into the bridge or tailpiece of an electric guitar and controlled by a metal bar or lever, that can produce gentle pitch fluctuations – and sometimes more dramatic 'detuning' effects!

Index